Edible Plants for Prairie Gardens

The Best Fruits, Vegetables and Herbs

... FOR LARRY, CHLOE, AND LAUREL, WITH LOVE.

Edible Plants for Prairie Gardens

The Best Fruits, Vegetables and Herbs

June Flanagan

FIFTH
HOUSE

3 5 7 9 10 8 6 4 2

Published by
Fifth House Ltd.
A Fitzhenry & Whiteside Company
195 Allstate Parkway
Markham, ON L3R 4T8
www.fifthhousepublishers.ca

Cover and interior design by BookWorks
Edited by Penny Hozy
Photographs by June Flanagan (except where noted)
Printed in Hong Kong

Fifth House Ltd. acknowledges, with thanks, the Canada Council for the Arts, and the Ontario Arts Council for their support of our publishing program. We acknowledge the financial support of the Government of Canada through the Canada Book Fund for our publishing activities.

 Canada Council Conseil des Arts
for the Arts du Canada

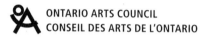 ONTARIO ARTS COUNCIL
CONSEIL DES ARTS DE L'ONTARIO

Library and Archives Canada Cataloguing in Publication
Flanagan, June
Edible plants for prairie gardens : the best fruits, vegetables and herbs / June Flanagan.
Includes index.
ISBN 978-1-897252-20-8
1. Fruit-culture–Prairie Provinces. 2. Fruit-culture–Great Plains.
3. Vegetable gardening–Prairie Provinces. 4. Vegetable gardening–Great
Plains. 5. Herb gardening–Prairie Provinces. 6. Herb gardening–Great
Plains. I. Title.
SB434.3.F53 2011   635.09712   C2011-904582-3

Publisher Cataloging-in-Publication Data (U.S)
Flanagan, June.
Edible plants for prairie gardens : the best fruits, vegetables and herbs / June Flanagan.
240 p. : col. photos. ; cm.
Includes index.
Summary: For gardeners in the Canadian Prairie Provinces and the Northern Great
Plains of the United States, this book shows how to grow fabulous fruits, vegetables
and herbs, including heirloom vegetables and new fruits bred especially for the prairies.
ISBN-13: 978-1-89725-220-8 (pbk.)
1. Gardening–Prairie Provinces. I. Title.
635.029 dc22   SB451.36.C3F536 2011

Acknowledgements

Many people deserve credit for helping me create this book. I am very grateful for the support my family gave me during its production.

I sincerely appreciate the people associated with Fifth House Publishers and Fitzhenry & Whiteside Limited for their collective talents that made this project polished and possible. With much gratitude, I thank Meaghan Craven, Charlene Dobmeier, Penny Hozy, Lesley Reynolds, Fraser Seely, and Stephanie Stewart.

The content was greatly enhanced by professionals who contributed their time to answer horticultural questions, supply images or lead me to more information. Thank you to Ken Allan, Karen Barby, Mark Benson, Jean Berezan, Elisabeth Beaubien, Bob Bors, Boughen Nursery, Paul de Jonge, Arden Delidais, Doug Edgar, Ieuan Evans, Gloria Gingera, Daniel Heaney, Jeffries Nursery, David Jensen, Jim Luco, Ron McMullin, Barbara Ramp, Line Rochefort, Philip Ronald, Rick Sawatzky, Gail Smith, Richard St-Pierre, Jim Ternier, Greg Wingate, Doug Waterer, and Raymond Winberg.

The text has been enriched with the experiences of prairie gardeners and growers who shared favourite plant varieties, growing and preserving tips, plants, seeds, photographs, bountiful harvests, refreshments, and recipes. They kept me posted on what was growing, blooming and producing, and opened their gardens and growing operations for photographs. With much appreciation, I thank Shalin Abbott, Shelly Barclay, Albert Bouw, Erin Bright, Geri Budd, Edna-Marie Caruso, Mary Caruso, John Chiste, Helena Danyk, Dick deBoer, Penny Dodd, Gwen Dorchak, Marian Dormaar, Keith Dudley, Lloyd Flaig, Donna Fremont, Carol Frouws, Fumiko, Jim George, Bob Gergely, Keaton Gibbs, Enid Gom, Ed Gouw and Marion Van Peer-Gouw, Barbara Boulton-Gunn and Kim Gunn, Elaine Harrison, Carol Johansen, Katie and Alan Johnston, Don McKay, Cathy J. Meyer, Anne and Nick Myshok, Rosina and Nick Mucciarone, Joanne and Morris Pashkowich, Allayna Ramp, William Ramp, Susan Rich, Tony Rich, Wayne and Rose Schellhorn, Brigitte Smith, Mike and Edith Stefancsik, Tracy and Kevin Saxon, Anna Stys, Nobby Sudo, and Karen Zanewich.

I also appreciated the opportunity to photograph at DNA Gardens, Fort Calgary, the Devonian Botanic Garden, Harvest Haven Market Farm, Lethbridge Grow It! Community Garden, and the Canadian National Institute for the Blind Fragrant Garden in Calgary.

Contents

CHAPTER ONE

Planning the Edible Garden

Why Grow Your Own?

Imagine having a fresh supply of fragrant herbs and organic fruits and vegetables all summer long, right on your doorstep. Nothing compares to the mouth-watering flavour of garden produce ripened on the tree or vine. With the information in this book, you can gain the satisfaction of growing your own. Homegrown edibles bring a personal touch to what's served on the table, and when it comes to eating locally, your garden is as close as it gets.

In addition to getting prime quality, gardeners who grow their own produce have more choice. Peek into any seed catalogue and discover a cornucopia of purple carrots, candy-cane striped beets, round cucumbers, golden raspberries, and cherry tomatoes that resemble miniature yellow pears. The options for your harvest basket go far beyond what's available at the supermarket.

This book will show you how to grow the best fruits, vegetables, and herbs for gardens in the Canadian Prairies and the Northern Great Plains of the United States. Written for new and experienced gardeners, it explains everything you need to know to produce a bountiful harvest, along with tips for saving your own seeds. You will also find advice for creating a garden of any size that appeals to all the senses, from a medley of potted herbs to your first vegetable patch to an urban landscape composed entirely of edibles.

Across Alberta to Manitoba, through Montana to Minnesota, prairie gardeners face frigid winters, fickle springs, drought, wind, and a fleeting number of frost-free days. In spite of unpredictable weather, harsh winters limit the number of insect pests to contend with and the arid climate reduces disease problems, which makes it easier to grow an organic garden. Long summer days

'Bright Lights' chard

'Touchstone Gold' and 'Detroit Dark Red' beets

partly compensate for our short growing season, and the combined effect of warm sunshine and cool nights, which has been described as "northern vigour," enhances the quality and flavour of many edibles, making the harvest very sweet.

In a short growing season, it matters which plants you choose and how you grow them. The prairie plant palette is rapidly expanding, and between these pages you'll discover the latest fruit and vegetable releases as well as heirloom varieties. When there wasn't enough room to include all possible crops, it reinforced my belief that we have plenty to pick from. In addition to being up-to-date, the plant descriptions and regionally adapted gardening practices are grouped in a unique format that will help you plan and plant. Step-by-step instructions describe how to raise seasonal produce, as well as long-lived edible plants that could grace your garden for many years.

'Royal Burgundy', yellow wax, and green beans

'Purple Haze' carrots

While gathering information, I realized how much prairie gardens reflect the diverse tastes of our rich multi-cultural heritage, as gardeners from many backgrounds introduced me to edibles they grew to make special dishes. Plants that are essential to traditional dishes from around the world have been wo-

ven into the text, and since an edible garden experience seems incomplete without sharing a few recipes, simple suggestions for serving and preserving your harvest are included with the plant descriptions.

Edible gardens are especially steeped in nostalgia as fond memories are built around meals that are prepared with homegrown food. My passion for nurturing edible plants began at an early age, while foraging for sweet strawberries and marvelling at swallowtail butterflies flitting on the curly parsley in my mother's garden. I witnessed nature's cycles firsthand as we

'Yellow Pear' tomatoes

collected seeds from our plants and watched them sprout and blossom the following year. To this day, heading out to the garden to gather something fresh for the table is a pleasure I couldn't do without.

Organic Gardening

This book emphasizes organic gardening practices, but what does that mean? Commercial growers have to meet strict standards to become certified organic, but for the home gardener, organic gardening is usually more loosely interpreted, and mainly it assumes that you are growing your produce without using pesticides. It also implies that you are replenishing your soil with organic matter so that it can support future crops without becoming depleted. These two premises underscore all the information in this book. My intention is to provide you with effective growing practices that are environmentally sound to help you raise nutritious produce from your garden.

Botany for Gardeners

Throughout the text, you will encounter many botanical terms. These words are not used in everyday language, but they appear in seed catalogues and on plant

Lettuce is a fast-growing annual plant.

Dramatic rhubarb sprouts each year from a perennial crown of roots.

Biennial cabbage is grown as an annual vegetable.

labels and they describe distinct plant characteristics. The characteristics often determine whether the plant is a good candidate for your garden, so the terms are included and explained to help you make informed choices. Before planning your edible garden, it's useful to know the meaning of terms defined here.

Vegetables, herbs, and flowers that are started from seed each spring and cleared from the garden at the end of the season are annuals and biennials.

Annual plants germinate, grow, flower, produce seed, and die in a single growing season. The frost-free period on the prairies isn't long enough for all crops to produce, which is why some gardeners go to great lengths to extend it.

Biennial plants germinate and grow the first year, and they die back to a crown of roots during the first winter. The second year, these plants re-sprout from the roots, produce flowers and seed during the growing season, and die. Most biennial garden crops, like carrots, are harvested the season they are planted, so gardeners may never see them flower, but this trait affects seed saving.

Perennials are non-woody plants that emerge from a crown of roots each spring, produce flowers and seed, and then die back to the crown at the end of the season. Unlike annuals, perennials re-sprout every year, if they are hardy enough to survive prairie winters. Hardy perennial edibles encompass vegetables

Warm-season tomatoes thrive in summer heat.

Woody plants include fruit trees Like this 'Gemini' apple tree. PHOTO - JEFFRIES NURSERY

UNDERSTANDING PLANT NAMES

The plants in this book are listed by their scientific and common names. Common names vary from place to place, but the scientific name for an individual species is the same all over the world. Knowing a plant's scientific name is useful when you want to learn more about it, collect seed from it, or source it for your garden.

The scientific name of a plant has two parts, which are written in italics or underlined. For example, *Petroselinum crispum* is the species name for parsley. If varieties or subspecies of a plant occur naturally, the variety name is listed in italics after the abbreviation "var." or "ssp." *Petroselinum crispum* var. *neapolitanum* is Italian flat-leaf parsley, while *Petroselinum crispum* var. *crispum* is curly parsley.

If the variety was developed through cultivation practices such as breeding or selection, it's called a "cultivar," which is a contraction of "cultivated variety." The terms cultivar and variety are often used interchangeably. Cultivars are named when a crop shows distinct inherited traits. The cultivar follows the scientific name, and is capitalized and in single quotes. Seed and plant catalogues usually list edible plants by common name and cultivar. As an example, 'Yukon Gold' potato is much easier to talk about than *Solanum tuberosum* ssp. *tuberosum* 'Yukon Gold.'

Related plants are grouped in families, and members of the same family often share similar cultivation requirements and are troubled by the same pests and diseases. To plan crop rotations it's essential to know which family an edible plant belongs to. Plant family names are capitalized and end in "*aceae*"; for example, *Fabaceae* is the bean family.

Scientists occasionally disagree on names, and names have changed as more sophisticated methods are developed to study plant relationships. This book attempts to use the most contemporary, commonly accepted scientific names for each of the plants described.

like asparagus, many herbs, and several small fruits such as rhubarb, strawberries, and raspberries.

Annual, biennial, and perennial plants from all over the world fall into two broad groups based on the temperature range in which they germinate and actively grow. *Cool-season* plants grow best when temperatures are about 15°C to 24°C (60°F to 75°F), while *warm-season* plants grow better at temperatures that range from about 27°C to 35°C (80°F to 95°F). Knowing which category a plant belongs to gives you an idea of when to plant it and what growing conditions it needs. Many cool-season edibles are cultivated for their leaves or roots, like lettuce and beets, and they generally grow well in prairie gardens. Warm-season edibles that are grown for fruit, such as eggplant and melons, often require extra effort from the gardener to satisfactorily produce in the prairie climate.

Edible *woody plants* are made up of fruit trees and fruiting shrubs. Temperature affects woody plants too, but they are generally classified according to hardiness zones rather than as cool-season or warm-season plants.

The *growing season* is the number of frost-free days between the last spring frost and the first fall frost. Weather data from your region will indicate the average frost dates. It's essential to choose plants and plant varieties that can produce within your growing season.

Getting Started

The first step in planning your edible garden is to determine whether you want to establish seasonal or permanent plantings, or both, and the difference is explained here.

This seasonal garden includes scarlet runner beans, tomatillos and squash.

Perennials such as rhubarb, chives and strawberries are candidates for a permanent garden.

The **seasonal garden** is made up of vegetables and herbs that must be replanted every year. Your seasonal garden may consist of just a few potted plants, but it's treated the same as a plot of land, because the plants die at the end of the season. The number of frost-free days in your area determines how long the seasonal garden exists, and it's critical to choose cultivars that can produce within that time.

The **permanent garden** contains long-term plant investments, such as fruit trees and fruiting shrubs. These woody plants take longer to produce, but if properly cared for, they become enduring fixtures. Perennial herbs, asparagus, rhubarb, strawberries, and raspberries are also considered permanent because they re-sprout every spring. Your permanent garden may only include a gooseberry bush, or a few herbs for making tea, but permanent plants have different needs than seasonal plants and should be in a separate area.

A practical plan places similar kinds of plants together so that it's easier to take care of them. Trees and large shrubs should be planted in one area, small shrubs and perennials in another, and it's best to incorporate annual vegetables and herbs in their own spot.

For the remainder of this book, the information is organized in the same way the plants should be arranged, in either the seasonal or permanent garden. That way, it's easier to plan and plant, as well as to maintain and harvest your edibles.

Defining Your Outdoor Space

It's important to decide how you want to use your outdoor space, and to balance your requirements with the needs of your plants. Begin by determining how much light is available; designate the sunniest sites for planting and reserve shaded spots for eating or play areas. Most fruits and vegetables grow best in full sun, which means they need more than six hours of direct light each day. A place that receives four to six hours of sunlight is described as being in partial shade, and if it gets less than four hours, it's in shade. Tall plants should be planted on the north side of the garden to avoid shading shorter ones.

Fruit trees like this 'Dolgo' crabapple put on a spectacular spring display.

Decide whether lawn will be part of your garden, and if so, how much and what shape. A patch of grass can be a transition from a deck to a vegetable border, highlighting the shapes of both areas, and it can provide a clean path to transport your fresh pickings. Or the lawn could be replaced with a cozy patio, surrounded by plantings of salad ingredients.

This inviting garden combines edibles with a beautiful flower border.

A vegetable and fruit border is attractive as well as edible.

There is no reason to limit your edibles to the back yard. Why not introduce your front entrance with a large, sweeping border of fragrant herbs or a showy fruit tree?

The shape of the beds around your plants sets the style of your garden. Large, simple shapes are visually more effective and easier to manage than intricate, small ones. Geometric shapes forge a formal look, while curving lines present an informal appearance that softens the sharp lines of buildings and walls to create a more relaxed environment.

Before you create a new planting bed, it's useful to visualize it by outlining its shape with a hose or rope. Stand back and evaluate it from inside the house or down the street. If possible, get a bird's-eye view by looking down on it from an upstairs window to determine if the shapes are pleasing and in proportion with the rest of the landscape.

Most edibles grow best in well-drained soil, which means that excess water drains rather than puddles as the soil becomes saturated. A raised bed provides better drainage and warms up faster in spring, but it requires more frequent watering than one at ground level.

Once you have evaluated your outdoor space as a whole, the next step is to define seasonal or permanent growing areas and to determine their size and shape.

Designing the Seasonal Garden

Seasonal plantings present great design opportunities, as it's relatively easy to combine small vegetables and herbs in areas that are outlined by bold or whimsical shapes, and each spring provides a clean canvas to renew your creativity. A sense of order can be established by grouping plants of the same type together, or by repeating plants at regularly spaced intervals. A mass of any kind makes an impressive show.

If symmetry appeals to you, consider building a simple "four square" design, where four square or rectangular planting beds are divided by perpendicular paths, and place a round feature, like a barrel of edible flowers or a sundial, in the centre where the paths meet. Within the beds, your edibles can be lined up in formal rows, or planted intensively in blocks that cover the soil.

Develop your planting area so it's easy to care for and harvest, with a nearby irrigation source and room to manoeuvre a wheelbarrow. The shape and size of your beds should be designed so that you can reach the centre to tend your plants without stepping on the soil.

Warm-season plants absolutely need full sun. Cool-season crops grow well in full sun, although many will do fine in partial shade. Arrange plants by their growing needs first, and then consider their aesthetic value. Leaf crops usually complement root crops and short rosettes look great beside upright stalks.

Raised beds create an accessible seasonal garden.

The broad foliage of bush beans complements slender onion leaves.

The seasonal garden is in a state of constant and rapid change, and edging can help it look permanent and intentional, even when the planting is not at its peak. Include annual edible flowers to spill into spaces as vegetables are pulled, or add a garden ornament. Obelisks are useful plant supports that look attractive even when they are unadorned.

Container Edibles: A surprising number of edible plants grow beautifully in pots, and a collection of them can convert a balcony, rooftop, or courtyard into a delightful oasis. Cultivars that form compact plants, which are perfect for containers, have been developed for almost every crop in the seasonal garden.

A big advantage of containers is their mobility; you can arrange them on steps, around a doorway, or on a patio. Container plants can be put out earlier in spring, kept out longer in fall, and covered or whisked inside when frost threatens. In a sunny location, the soil in pots warms quickly, which is conducive to warm-season plants like basil and eggplant. Planted pots require less physical work than garden beds and can be positioned at a comfortable height that allows the gardener to plant, water, and harvest without bending over.

Fragrant mint is a desirable container plant.

Edible flowers such as nasturtiums add colour to the seasonal garden.

Even the smallest outdoor space can accommodate an aromatic collection, as herbs rank among the best container plants of all the edibles. Their ornamental foliage makes it easy to create an attractive display, and their fragrance permeates the surroundings as you brush past them.

The best candidates for your pots are the same plants that make up the seasonal garden. Select varieties bred especially for container growing such as bush tomatoes, compact cucumbers, and dwarf peas, or provide a support for vine types so they can grow vertically. Edible flowers can be added for a splash of colour. If there is enough space, it's fine to combine plants, but it's better not to mix cool-season plants and warm-season plants in the same container.

Small perennial herbs and day-neutral strawberries can be grown in containers, although these won't survive the winter outdoors unless the entire pot is sunk in the ground.

COMPANION PLANTS

• •

Popular garden literature that lists companion plants that "like each other" is usually rooted in folklore that is more fun than fact. While some beneficial plant associations have been proven, it's unnecessary to complicate your design by fretting over particular combinations. It's more important to create a diverse planting, as it attracts a variety of pollinators and predators that keep pests in check. A mixed collection of plants also disrupts the ability of insect pests to find their preferred plants for feeding or laying eggs.

Early-maturing vegetable cultivars are most likely to succeed in our short growing season.

Determinate bush beans such as 'Venture' produce earlier than vine types.

Choosing Edibles for the Seasonal Garden

In addition to well-stocked garden centres, there is an abundance of inspiring printed and online seed catalogues, illustrated with images of plump produce. Browsing catalogue offerings is a wonderful way to spend the winter, dreaming about the promise of spring. These listings provide cultivar descriptions and growing information to help you plan your garden. The following characteristics should be considered when deciding which plants to choose for your seasonal garden.

Days to Maturity: It's critical to grow cultivars that can produce within your growing season, and the best guideline for determining which cultivar is appropriate is to check the number of days it takes to reach maturity. It's also important to know whether the figure is based on planting it outdoors from seed or as a transplant.

Many crops require a certain accumulation of heat over the season to mature, and different cultivars of the same crop can mature at different times. In addition, the dramatic change in day-length at northern latitudes affects the way plants develop, and there are large swings in temperature at the beginning and

Indeterminate 'Scarlet Runner' bean vines can completely cover a trellis.

end of the season. Since the days to maturity are determined in regions with less variation, it's a good idea to add thirty days to the figure when you are deciding whether a warm-season cultivar will produce within the frost-free period in your garden.

Vines vs. Bush Plants (Indeterminate vs. Determinate): Several vegetable crops, including peas, beans, tomatoes, cucumbers, and squash are produced on two types of plants; their growth form and eventual size is genetically programmed, regardless of how much you water or fertilize them. In addition to determining how much space the plant needs, these growth forms influence when the crop ripens and how much it produces.

Bush plants are known as determinate; they grow to a predetermined size and produce one crop of flowers and fruit at the end of the stems. Since the plants are smaller, bush types reach maturity faster and produce earlier crops than vines, and suit short growing seasons. All the fruits ripen near the same time, so these types are desirable when a large quantity is needed for processing. For example, determinate tomato cultivars are ideal for making sauce.

Vines are indeterminate plants that grow to a certain stage before production begins, and then continue to grow and produce until frost. The fruits form and ripen in sequence as the vine grows, and their staggered ripening results in a continuous harvest, rather than a large quantity at once. As an example, indeterminate cultivars are ideal when you want an ongoing supply of tomatoes for salads or sandwiches.

Bush types are space conserving, but vine types can fit in small areas if they are grown vertically.

Heirloom and Open-Pollinated Seeds: Seeds have been handed down throughout history, since plants were first cultivated. As people collected seeds from the earliest, hardiest, tastiest, and most productive plants to grow the next season's crop, the seeds became a lifeline from one year to another. Every seed captured a legacy acquired through its ancestors, and over time, many plants were domesticated with remarkable modifications.

If you wish to save seeds from your plants, it's best to choose open-pollinated cultivars. The seeds from these crops produce plants that maintain recognizable characteristics in each generation when they are naturally pollinated. Open-pollinated plants contain traits that contribute to a diverse gene pool. When you grow and save their seeds, you might be preserving a genetic tool set for meeting future environmental challenges, such as climate change or disease.

Determinate paste tomatoes make excellent container plants.

Heirlooms are open-pollinated cultivars that have been cherished for at least fifty years, and their descriptive names often hint at the plant's history. Most vegetable heirlooms originated before the 1950s, when hybrid seeds became widely available.

Hybrid seeds: Hybrids can occur in nature, but commercially produced hybrid seeds are developed under highly controlled conditions. Specific traits from parent plants are combined in their seeds, with the goal of producing uniform plants that possess the chosen characteristics. Hybrids are usually labelled with the designation "F1," which indicates first-generation offspring. Hybrid seeds are expensive because the breeding requires hand pollination, segregated space, and a long time to produce desirable results.

COMMUNITY GARDENS

If you live in an apartment or condominium, or if garden space is lacking where you live, consider joining or initiating a community garden. Community gardens have been established in cities across North America, making it possible for many people to enjoy the pleasure of planting. In addition to providing a place to cultivate a piece of earth, the opportunity exists to exchange ideas, solve problems and share experiences with other gardeners. Some community gardens are structured to host educational programs, coordinate group gardening activities, supply tools, or provide composting facilities. Building a garden on common ground is a great way to grow your own food and to connect with and foster a sense of pride within your community.

Community gardens provide a wonderful opportunity to grow food and exchange ideas.

Hybrids are often vigorous plants that have been developed for attributes such as compact growth, disease resistance, high yields, or early maturity. However, saving their seeds isn't recommended because the next generation of plants can have unpredictable characteristics.

Designing the Permanent Garden

It's possible to create a landscape that is engaging in all seasons and entirely edible when you choose food plants for your permanent garden. Use fruit trees and fruiting shrubs with showy spring blossoms and striking autumn colours to form the framework, and incorporate perennial herbs to transform ordinary earth into an extraordinary sensory experience. Classic plants with edible flowers such as roses, lilacs, and daylilies can further increase the diversity and allure of your food-producing setting.

The permanent garden deserves careful thought in the beginning, but long-lived edibles can be very rewarding, and less demanding than vegetables and herbs in the seasonal garden.

Large woody fruits make good anchors for the back or centre of a bed, with smaller fruits placed in front, toward the edges, or in their own bed. Select the placement of the tallest plants first, and shape your beds around them. Allow enough space for each plant to mature while receiving good air circulation and plenty of sunlight. In large beds, stepping-stones should be installed to access plants.

Situate fruits where it's less likely that they will break dormancy during warm winter weather or spring temperature swings, or during Chinook winds. The north side of a slope, building, or wall is preferable to the south, as a northern exposure warms up more slowly, and the plants are less likely to be affected by rapid changes in temperature. Avoid planting fruit trees or shrubs at the base of a slope, as this is where frost pockets form and also where water collects in spring. Locate them away from footpaths and driveways so their fruit drop won't be annoying.

Place culinary herbs close to the kitchen for convenience, or around a patio or deck where their aromatic leaves can perfume the air. Low-growing herbs make exceptional edging between stepping-stones and along pathways.

A patch of raspberries will reward you with mouth-watering sweet fruit.

Consider hardiness, disease resistance, size, pollination requirements, and fruit characteristics when choosing cultivars.

Plants with edible flowers like the 'Morden Blush' rose suit the spirit of an edible garden.

Most perennial edibles such as herbs and rhubarb are easiest to care for in a bed composed solely of perennials, and usually one plant of each type is sufficient. The exceptions include asparagus, strawberries, and raspberries, where a patch of several plants of each type is cultivated in order to harvest an adequate crop.

Choosing Edibles for the Permanent Garden

The prairie climate limits which fruits we can grow, but compared to what was available for previous generations, prairie gardeners now have a fair amount of choice, and research is ongoing to expand it. For the past century, ambitious growers and scientists on the prairies have been combining the gene pool of the hardiest wild fruits with the sweetest cultivated ones to produce increased hardiness, improved disease resistance, better storage quality, and fine-tasting, larger fruit. This work has yielded unique cultivars that bear nutritionally rich fruits with complex, concentrated flavours.

Hardiness, disease resistance, the mature size of the plant, and the characteristics of the fruit are factors to consider when choosing fruit cultivars. It's also critical to know whether more than one plant is necessary for cross-pollination in order to produce fruit, and if the fruit will mature within your growing season.

Hardiness, disease resistance, and the amount of space required to produce a crop are important considerations when choosing which perennial edibles to grow.

The 'Evan's sour cherry features colourful fall foliage.

In this book, the plants that are described for the permanent garden are prairie-hardy, but not all cultivars are hardy in all locations. Some urban areas are large enough to create their own microclimates, which makes it possible to grow cultivars that require shelter in surrounding rural areas. Hardiness has not been thoroughly tested in all cultivars, but those that are described as moderately hardy are known to grow well in zone 3, using the Canadian Plant Hardiness Zones map, and the cultivars rated as very hardy are usually appropriate for zone 2.

HARDINESS ZONES

Hardiness zone systems have been developed in Canada and the United States to predict which plants will survive in an area, but each system uses different climate data and numbering so comparisons between them are not straightforward. The USDA system was revised in 1990, and is based solely on minimum winter temperatures. In addition to minimum winter temperatures, the Canadian system incorporates length of the growing season, snow depth, precipitation, maximum temperatures, and wind data. The Canadian map was updated in 2000 with recent climate information and the effect of elevation. The systems were designed to evaluate woody plants, but the ratings are often applied to perennial plants, too.

In 2004, Natural Resources Canada took the Canadian Plant Hardiness Zones map a step further in an ongoing program titled *Going Beyond the Zones*, where the potential range of an individual species can be mapped based on its survival in different locations.

For hardiness information visit these Web sites:
Canadian map: <http://planthardiness.gc.ca>
United States map: <http://usna.usda.gov/Hardzone/>

Finally ...

Be sure to designate a place to rest and experience the pleasures of your edible garden. Hang a hammock or swing, or settle a chaise lounge under an apple tree, among the herbs, or near the vegetable patch, in a setting where you can sample your first pickings, fresh from the source.

EDIBLE FLOWERS

Edible flowers suit the spirit of a food-producing garden and can supply you with blossoms to embellish salads and desserts and serving plates. Their petals are usually considered the palatable part, although they can be an acquired taste, and most are valued more for decoration than flavour.

Before eating any flower, be absolutely sure you have identified it correctly and know that it is edible, as similar plants can be poisonous. For example, garden peas are edible, while sweet peas are not. Only eat flowers that are known to be free of pesticides; never consume flowers from a florist or from purchased plants until they produce new growth in your garden. Especially use caution when sampling flowers if you have a pollen allergy or asthma.

Prepare edible blossoms by gently immersing them in water and removing any insects. Allow them to dry before arranging them on desserts or as a garnish. To add flowers to a salad, gently pull off the petals and discard the other flower parts. Petals are fragile and wilt quickly; reserve them for the final touch and add them just before serving. Most culinary herbs have edible blossoms, although they can be intensely aromatic and should be used sparingly.

Cultivate edible flowers using the same gardening practices as other edible plants, in a location with enough sunlight and plenty of space to grow. Combine plants with similar needs, allocating blooming woody plants and perennials to your permanent garden and annual flowers in your seasonal garden.

Suggested Edible Flowers for the Permanent Garden:

Woody Plants

Apple (*Malus* sp.) – all cultivars

Lilac (*Syringa* sp.) – all cultivars

Rose (*Rosa* sp.) – all cultivars

Perennial Plants

Clove pinks (*Dianthus caryophyllus* or *Dianthus plumarius*)

Daylily (*Hemerocallis* sp.) – all cultivars

English lavender (*Lavendula angustifolia* 'Munstead')

Wild bergamot (*Monarda fistulosa*)

Suggested Edible Flowers for the Seasonal Garden:

Borage (*Borago officinalis*)

Calendula (*Calendula officinalis*)

Nasturtium (*Tropaeolum majus*)

Pansy (*Viola wittrockiana*)

Viola (*Viola tricolor*)

Calendula

Borage

Pansy

Wild bergamot

Daylily

Nasturtium

Lilac

Clove pinks

English lavender 'Munstead'

Viola

CHAPTER TWO

Planting the Edible Garden

Soil

Soil anchors a plant's roots and supplies them with water, air, and nutrients. It also houses a complex web of bacteria, fungi, earthworms, spiders, and insects. Much of the teeming life underground is sustained by decomposing plant parts, such as fallen autumn leaves. The decomposition process creates organic matter that eventually returns nutrients back to the soil in a beautifully integrated system that generates new plants to repeat the cycle.

Along with decomposed organic matter, known as humus, soil is made up of particles of weathered minerals, and the size of the particles determines soil texture. Sand particles are large and rounded, clay particles are tiny and flat, and silt particles are smaller than sand but larger than clay. The spaces between particles, called pores, allow movement of air, water, plant roots, and other soil creatures. Humus acts like a sponge and natural glue between soil particles; it absorbs and holds water and nutrients and it binds particles together in clumps, which creates pore space.

Most prairie soils tend to be mostly sand or clay. Sandy soils contain large pores that are well aerated, but water drains rapidly through them, washing nutrients away. Clay particles hold nutrients tightly, and the small pores between them drain slowly and hold little air. Humus improves both kinds of soils; it provides better aeration and drainage in clay soils, and helps hold nutrients and water in sandy soils.

Another important soil characteristic is its degree of acidity, known as pH. The pH affects whether certain essential nutrients are available in a form that plants can use, and it's measured on a scale of 0 to 14, where 7 is neutral. A low pH value indicates a more acidic soil; alkaline soils have higher values. The

Soil supports plants and a complex web of life underground.

Autumn leaves decompose and return organic matter to the soil.

range where most plant nutrients can be readily absorbed lies between a pH of 6 and 7. In areas with low precipitation such as the prairies, the pH tends to be high, although there are exceptions. Some plants, such as blueberries, are very sensitive to pH; they cannot extract essential nutrients in alkaline soils and don't grow well on the prairies. Alkaline soils can be moderated somewhat by the addition of organic matter and sulphur, but it's difficult to significantly change them. In acidic soils, lime is usually added to make conditions more favourable for plant growth.

Before creating your edible garden, it's a good idea to have your soil tested by a regional soil-testing lab to find out whether it contains what your plants need. If amendments are necessary, it's much easier to incorporate them before you plant. A soil test provides valuable information about texture, pH, and organic matter content as well as the nutrient status and whether problems such as salinity exist. Once you gather background information from an initial soil test, it's advisable to update it every three to five years to make informed decisions about maintaining your soil.

Preparing the Soil

The best thing you can do for your soil is to imitate nature and add organic matter to it, and a good source comes from decomposed yard and kitchen waste, known as compost. Compost will sustain the life beneath your soil and provide nutrition slowly and naturally to your plants as decomposers break it down. In addition, compost recycles plant waste that would otherwise contribute to landfills.

Other sources of organic matter include autumn leaves, straw, sawdust, and wood chips, but these materials should be composted before adding them to your soil, because decomposers require a certain amount of nitrogen to break them down. If you dig these sources directly into your garden, they borrow nitrogen from the soil, which makes it temporarily unavailable to your plants. Composted material should be aged for at least six months before using it around edible plants. Well-aged compost from livestock manure and municipal waste are appropriate for amending soil, but use them conservatively, as both can be high in salts that are harmful to plants. Never apply fresh manure to your garden; it will burn your plants and contains bacteria that pose a health hazard.

To create a new planting area in your

Compost recycles kitchen and yard waste.

seasonal vegetable garden, apply compost, 1 to 2.5 cm (0.5 to 1 in.) deep across the bed, and incorporate it into the soil to a depth of 15 to 30 cm (6 to 12 in.). Level the planting area with a hard rake, and avoid compacting the prepared soil by not stepping on it. Minimize cultivation after preparing your soil as it increases the rate of decomposition and moisture loss, disturbs soil creatures, and contributes toward breakdown of the soil structure.

Organic matter continually breaks down, so your seasonal garden should be replenished with it each year. Prepare existing beds for planting by spreading a 1 cm (0.5 in.) layer of compost across them and work it in to a depth of 15 cm (6 in.), or simply leave the compost spread evenly across the surface as a top-dressing, where it acts as a mulch and slowly becomes incorporated into the soil as it decomposes.

When you plant a new area of your permanent garden with perennial vegetables, herbs, or small fruits, apply compost in the same way as described for your seasonal garden. It's unnecessary to add compost to the soil before planting fruiting shrubs and fruit trees unless a soil test indicates a need; as explained later in this chapter, it's better to maintain the soil around these deeply rooted plants with a heavy-textured mulch.

Composting

Home composting is an excellent way to recycle your kitchen scraps, grass clippings, spent garden plants, and autumn leaves into moist, crumbly dark humus for your garden. Get started by choosing an outdoor location for your pile; it will decompose faster and thaw earlier in spring if it's in a sunny spot, but a shaded pile is easier to keep moist. Determine whether you'll contain your compost in a commercial bin or a homemade frame, and situate the pile in direct contact with the soil for a ready source of decomposers, or add a shovelful of compost or soil to get it started. To keep vermin out, enclose it with wire mesh and cover it, or use a commercial bin.

Collect vegetable and fruit peels and cores, used coffee grounds, tea leaves, egg shells, autumn leaves, and spent garden plants for your pile. Add grass clippings if no herbicides have been used on your lawn. Don't add meat or dairy products, grease, pet droppings, or pest-infested plants as these attract vermin or carry disease. Wood ashes are fine for the pile, but not charcoal ashes. Yard waste should be shredded or chipped to expose more surface area to microorganisms so that the pieces break down faster.

Decomposition will eventually happen, but it happens faster when the pile is about 1 cubic metre (1 cubic yard) in size, and contains a mixture of moist green and dry brown plant parts. Green waste includes kitchen scraps, cut flowers, freshly pulled weeds, sod pieces, and grass clippings. Dry brown waste is made up of autumn leaves, wood ashes, straw, bark, wood chips, and sawdust. Soil bacteria need a certain ratio of carbon to nitrogen; juicy green materials are higher in nitrogen and decompose faster than dry brown pieces, which are much higher in carbon. Dry pieces help fluff up the pile so that air can circulate through it.

To maintain a prime environment for soil creatures to do their work, keep your pile moist like a damp sponge and turn it weekly during the growing season with a digging fork to aerate it. A pile that smells is either too wet, too compacted, or has too much green waste and not enough dry stuff. Cover your pile with a tarp to conserve moisture, as decomposition will slow down if the

Two styles of compost bins, one constructed of wood and the other a purchased plastic bin.

pile dries out. A cover also helps prevent nutrients from being washed away when it rains or snows.

In winter, it's fine to add kitchen scraps to the compost pile, even when it is frozen. Just resume stirring the ingredients when the pile thaws in spring.

Planting the Seasonal Garden
When to Plant

The popular tradition of planting the entire garden during the May holiday weekend yields satisfactory results with some crops, but better timing improves the performance of many more. Historically, gardeners relied on cues from nature to determine when to sow their seeds; now most gardeners plan their sowings around the date of the average last spring frost. Both methods work well, but a soil thermometer will help you fine-tune your plantings, because once moisture is available, soil temperature controls germination.

Planting by Frost Date or Soil Temperature: Cool-season plants should be sown or transplanted outdoors before the spring frost date; warm-season crops should

Fall-planted garlic and 'Buttercrunch' lettuce emerge early in spring.

Sow cool-season chard about two weeks before the average last spring frost date.

Plant warm-season beans near the date of the average last spring frost.

be planted after the likelihood of frost has passed. Cool-season plants can be split again into two groups: the hardiest bunch, which includes spinach and lettuce, can be planted as early as the soil can be worked; the remainder are planted about two weeks before the frost date. Warm-season plants can be split similarly: some, like beans, can be planted around the frost date, and others, such as eggplants or melons, do better in warmer soil and are usually planted two weeks later.

Cool-season plants can satisfy the desire to coax something green from the earth early in the season, as they germinate in soil temperatures as cool as 5°C to 7°C (41°F to 45°F). These plants germinate fastest when the air temperature is 13°C to 21°C (55°F to 70°F), and germination declines when air temperatures rise above 25°C (77°F). Many cool-season species tolerate a light frost, and the planting period usually runs from late April to mid May.

Warm-season species can be seeded or transplanted when the soil has warmed to 15°C to 18°C (60°F to 65°F), usually from late May through early June. These crops originate from hot climates and germinate fastest when soil temperatures are 21°C to 29°C (70°F to 85°F), and their seeds often rot when sown in cold soil.

Cues from nature: The average date of the last spring frost is a good guideline for scheduling your outdoor planting, but it's not a guarantee. Cues from nature are more closely synchronized to seasonal variations than the calendar and can help determine the best time to plant, especially as flowering and frost dates shift with climate change.

The common lilac (*Syringa vulgaris*) doesn't open its leaf and flower buds until it experiences a certain amount of accumulated heat in the air and soil. Depending on weather conditions, its bloom period can vary by three weeks, and it's a proven indicator of spring. As the lilac starts to leaf out, it's time to sow cool-season crops, and warm-season crops can be sown when the flowers are in full bloom. As lilac blossoms fade, it's usually safe to set out squash and cucumber transplants. Coordinate your planting schedule with the development of lilac shrubs that are growing in open areas, because those near south-facing walls bloom earlier.

Native prairie plants are useful to time spring plantings, too. Based on observations, lettuce and peas can be sown when golden beans (*Thermopsis rhombifolia*) flower; sow carrots, beets, and broad beans as saskatoons (*Amelanchier alnifolia*) bloom; and plant potatoes when poplar trees (*Populus* sp.) leaf out.

Effects of Temperature and Daylength: The arrival of summer causes some crops to bloom, which is also called "bolting" or "running to seed." A combination of temperature and day length influences flowering in many edible plants, and it frustrates gardeners because it can cause the flavour to become so bitter that the plants must be culled to the compost pile. Premature flowering is a problem with many cool-season crops on the prairies, where summer comes so rapidly on the heels of spring. To solve this problem, choose bolt-resistant cultivars, sow as early as possible in spring, or sow in late July so that the plants develop as nights get longer, or set out transplants of non-root crops in early May.

A period of temperatures between 5°C and 7°C (40°F to 45°F) can trigger biennial seedlings, like beets and cabbage, to bloom the first year. Even though these germinate in cool soil and tolerate frost, it's better to sow them no earlier

When native prairie plants such as golden bean flower, it's usually time to sow cool-season lettuce and peas.

Warm temperatures and long day lengths cause lettuce to bolt.

A cold snap can trigger biennial chicory seedlings to bloom prematurely.

than early May, choose bolt-resistant cultivars, or set out transplants of non-root crops close to the frost date to prevent premature bolting.

Succession Planting: Even in a short growing season, it's possible to plant more than one crop in the same spot in succession. One strategy is to replant the spot where you harvested an early spring crop with a fast-growing warm-season crop; just as spring radishes are pulled, the weather may be warm enough to transplant a fast-growing zucchini or to sow bush beans. Or, squeeze in two cool-season sowings for salads; sow mesclun greens in early spring and plant endive or lettuces in midsummer for fall pickings. Depending on how long each cultivar needs to mature, early peas can be followed by baby endive, broad beans by lettuce, or spinach by carrots.

Before planting the second crop, check the number of days it requires to reach maturity, and calculate whether it will produce adequately before the first frost in fall. Count backwards from the fall frost date, and allow time for germination and maturity plus at least two extra weeks to account for the shorter days and cooler temperatures that slow growth late in the season. Salad crops that will be harvested as baby greens can be planted up until six weeks before the first frost.

If your enthusiasm hasn't waned after the garden is cleaned up at the end

Warm-season zucchini will fill in after cool-season kale and Japanese bunching onions are harvested.

of the season, make another sowing of the hardiest crops to get early sprouts the following spring. Candidates that might succeed with this approach include spinach, carrots, peas, lettuce, and chicory; mesclun greens such as mizuna, arugula, mâche, and cress; and herbs like parsley, dill, and chervil. Sow these seeds in late fall, when it is too cold to germinate but before the ground freezes, usually in late October. In areas with severe winters, insulate your planting with a layer of mulch and remove the mulch in early spring so the soil warms faster.

Seeding and Transplanting Outdoors

When the soil is dry enough to be worked in spring, prepare your planting area so that it is weed-free, and apply compost, levelling it with a hard rake.

Most seeds should be sown about 0.5 to 1 cm (0.25 to 0.5 in.) deep; large seeds, like squash, should be sown 2.5 cm (1 in.) deep, and it's best to simply press tiny seeds into the soil surface and barely cover them. Germination of very small seeds is often promoted by light, which they will receive when they are close to the surface. Small seeds have limited food stores and if planted too deep, the seed will exhaust its reserves before the sprout reaches the surface. Seeds require oxygen for germination, and when planted at a depth that corresponds to their size, adequate oxygen should be available if the soil is not waterlogged.

During germination, the soil must be kept moist, but never soggy. Until germination occurs, it's a good idea to irrigate your planting with a nozzle or watering can that produces a fine spray or gentle shower so the seeds are not washed away.

Hardening Off Transplants: Before planting your seedlings in the garden, it's important to reduce their growth rate so they will adapt to outdoor conditions faster. This process is called "hardening off" and it's done by exposing the plant to lower temperatures or by reducing water.

Harden off your annual plants over a one- to two-week period. Initially, keep them irrigated, place them in a shaded area that is protected from wind, and bring them indoors at night. Gradually increase their exposure to cool temperatures, sun, and wind, and eventually leave them outdoors overnight, ready to transplant in the garden.

Harden off broccoli transplants before setting them outdoors.

Seedlings of biennial plants may bolt if they are exposed to temperatures of 5°C (42°F) for a period of time, so it's best to harden these off by withholding water, allowing them to become fairly dry between irrigations. Plant them in the garden closer to the frost date to reduce the risk of chilly temperatures that might cause bolting.

Choose a cloudy day or a cool evening to transplant seedlings that have been hardened off. Dig a hole twice as wide and as deep as the container. Handle the root ball carefully, and plant it at the same depth in the garden as it was in the container. Create a shallow basin around each plant to hold water and irrigate thoroughly after transplanting. Keep the soil evenly moist until new growth appears.

It's useful to keep a record of the cultivars you planted, with the dates they were seeded, transplanted, and harvested. Also note frost dates, precipitation, soil and air temperatures, and disease or insect problems. Over time, your records will help you plan your garden and determine which cultivars are best.

Planting Containers: Choose containers that are at least 30 cm (12 in.) in depth and diameter, with drainage holes. Terracotta pots are aesthetically pleas-

Seedlings require more frequent irrigation in terracotta pots than in plastic or ceramic containers.

ing, but they dry out faster than glazed ceramics or plastic. Large half-barrels and tubs can accommodate plants well, although they are difficult to move unless they rest on a wheeled trolley.

Garden soil and compost are acceptable in an outdoor planting mix; a classic mix includes equal parts of soil, coarse sand, and compost. If you use a soil-less mix, it's necessary to supply nutrients through a complete fertilizer, following the recommended rate on the package. Allow room in the container to apply mulch around your plants.

Container-grown edibles are planted at the same time as like plants in the garden, but their confined space requires more frequent irrigation and supplemental nutrition to produce quality crops.

Place the containers where your plants receive enough sun. The soil in pots warms up faster, which encourages earlier production from heat-loving plants.

At the end of the season, compost the spent plant parts and soil, and store empty pots in a covered location. Frost-proof containers can be filled with a decorative winter arrangement of dried branches and seed-heads while you contemplate what to grow in them next year.

Containers warm up quickly and encourage early production from heat-loving 'Salad Bush' cucumbers.

A cold frame collects heat, encouraging growth of warm-season tomato and basil plants.

Extending the Season

Warming the Soil: The garden can be planted earlier if you warm the soil. Dark compost mulch absorbs heat, but it's possible to raise the temperature higher under sheets of plastic. Plastic mulch isn't natural or aesthetically pleasing, but it collects solar heat and prevents evaporation of soil moisture.

Plastic mulch should be applied in early spring, two weeks before planting. Prepare the soil and irrigate it thoroughly; then stretch the plastic tight against the surface, securing the edges with soil, boards, or rocks. If you plan to irrigate with a drip system, install it before the plastic.

Three practical types of plastic mulch include clear, black, or IRT (infrared transmitting) sheets. Clear polyethylene produces the warmest soil, but weeds grow well under it, and the soil can get too hot for some crops if it's left in place after planting. Black doesn't warm the soil as much as clear does, but it blocks sunlight, so there is less of a weed problem. IRT plastic is a special item that is available through garden product suppliers. It lets certain wavelengths of light pass through to warm the soil without encouraging weed germination, and raises the soil temperature midway between what's achieved with black or clear plastic.

Clear polyethylene sheeting is also useful to hasten germination while the soil is still cool in spring. Cover the bed with it after sowing your seeds; stretch it tight against the soil surface and secure the edges. Remove it when the sprouts poke through the soil, or the heat will cook them.

Water-filled cones insulate tomato seedlings from frost.

Crop Covers and Frost Protection: The simplest method to protect your plants from frost is to cover them with a blanket. Cover them before sundown to retain warmth, and support the blanket with tomato cages or buckets so that it doesn't rest on the plants. A waterproof tarp can be placed over the blanket if moisture is in the forecast.

Clear crop covers are most useful to extend the growing season in spring when plants are small. They are designed to collect solar heat, provide wind protection, and raise humidity. Certain types also offer protection from frost.

Tomato seedling protected by a crop cover.

The water-filled cone remains in place as the tomato vine outgrows it.

A floating row cover supported over plants offers some frost protection.

Many gardeners combine crop covers with plastic mulch to increase warmth and to keep weeds down. Clear covers should be supported off plant leaves, and ventilated during the day to prevent over-heating. All crop covers must be removed if the temperature rises above 27°C (80°F). They must also be removed to allow pollination, unless you hand-pollinate. Covers that are made of clear or opaque plastic or single pane glass don't prevent heat loss at night, so these types should be covered with a blanket to protect your plants when frost is forecast. It's necessary to firmly secure covers in windy areas to prevent abrasion on the plants.

Commercially produced, water-filled, clear polyethylene cones are an effective method of protecting individual young plants from frost, and are often used when setting out tomatoes. The top can be opened during warm days, and kept open as the plant outgrows the cone.

For a few degrees of frost protection, it's handy to have a floating row cover, made from spun-bonded polyester. It's unattractive, but it's easy to install and is re-useable. The fabric allows sunlight and moisture to pass through, but it doesn't trap as much heat as clear materials and doesn't require ventilation. A floating row cover is light enough to be laid directly on the plants if it's held in place around the edges with soil, rocks, or boards, but it must be supported over tomatoes, peppers, cucumbers, and melons, as the growing points of these plants are easily damaged. Floating row covers are often used to envelop warm-season crops with heat for the first three or four weeks of the growing season. A lightweight version of the same material is useful as an insect barrier against pests or to produce a pure seed crop.

A cold frame is an unheated miniature greenhouse that is used to harden off transplants, to grow cool-season salad greens in early spring and fall, and to plant warm-season crops earlier in spring. The classic design is a bottomless wood frame with a clear, slanted top that faces south. A simpler cover can be fashioned from 9-gauge wire hoops, about 45 cm (18 in.) high, covered with a clear polyethylene sheet, and ventilated by rolling up the plastic sides.

Inexpensive crop covers can be made by wrapping the outside of a tomato cage with clear polyethylene sheets, leaving the top open for air movement, or by cutting the bottom off an opaque plastic milk jug. Remove the cap during the day for ventilation, and replace it before sundown to retain heat. Very small plants can be protected on frosty nights with Styrofoam cups.

Planting the Permanent Garden

Bare-root plants should be planted in early spring when the soil is dry enough to be worked; container-grown edibles can be planted throughout spring. Keep your potted perennials and woody fruits moist until you are ready to put them in the ground. The roots of bare-root plants should be soaked in a bucket of water.

Begin by raking the planting area level. It's unnecessary to cultivate or to amend the soil prior to planting fruit trees and fruiting shrubs, unless a soil test indicates otherwise, but it's a good idea to incorporate compost through-out the planting area where perennial plants are grown, as mentioned earlier in this chapter.

Make sure your designated planting location allows enough space on all sides for the plant to grow to maturity, taking care not to put it too close to a building or a fence. Dig a hole that is twice the diameter and the same depth as the container or root ball, and create a small mound in the centre of the plant-ing hole, to support the roots.

Spread the roots of bare-root or potted plants out in a radial fashion over the mound; untangle twisted or circling roots and prune damaged ones. The roots of pot-bound plants that circle the container should be spread out because they will increase in girth as the plant grows, and can eventually strangle the plant. If the planting mix looks or feels different than your soil, rinse it off the roots before planting, as water does not move readily through different soil types.

Install the plant so that its crown (the point where the stems or trunk and roots meet) is even with the soil surface, at the same level it was grown in the container. If the plant is a grafted fruit tree, install it so the graft union (a knob at the base of the trunk) is above the ground. Backfill the planting hole with the same soil that was removed. Some planting instructions still recommend adding organic matter to the planting hole, but long-term studies have shown that this causes trees and shrubs to struggle once their roots reach the limits of the pampered conditions inside the planting hole, and the roots may not venture further. Drainage and uneven drying also become problems between the two different types of soil.

Create a shallow 5 cm (2 in.) basin around the plant to hold water, out to the edge of its leaf canopy, and tamp the soil around the plant firmly. Irrigate immediately after planting by filling the basin slowly and allowing the water to soak in deeply.

Mulch the seasonal garden with organic material such as straw.

Mulch

Garden mulch mirrors a natural process, covering the soil surface with organic matter like a protective blanket. In nature, the spent leaves and plant parts that fall to the ground feed the decomposition cycle, and mulch works the same way in your garden.

Mulch has many desirable properties. It slows evaporation from the soil, inhibits the germination of weed seeds by blocking sunlight, insulates the soil, and moderates soil temperatures so that plants have better root growth in summer and fewer problems with frost heaving in winter. Mulch permits water to penetrate the soil slowly, reducing run-off and erosion, and it lessens the amount of soil splashed on leaves, which in turn decreases the incidence of soil-borne diseases and improves the plant's appearance. As it decomposes, mulch returns essential plant nutrients and organic matter to the soil. Mulch should be applied to every part of your edible garden as soon as it is planted.

Irrigate thoroughly before applying mulch in any area, and wet the mulch immediately after you apply it. It's not a good idea to use landscape fabric underneath, because it blocks organic matter and nutrients from being returned to the soil as the mulch breaks down.

In your seasonal garden and newly planted containers, spread a thin layer of mulch across the soil surface at planting, and increase the depth as seedlings grow. Compost, dried grass clippings, straw, and well-shredded leaves are good mulch materials to use around seasonal plants. In autumn, any recognizable materials can be turned into the soil, gathered and put in the compost pile, or

Mulch container-grown herbs to conserve water.

Mulch permanent plantings with wood chips.

used to protect perennial plants over winter. Wood chips are not appropriate for the seasonal garden, except on container-grown plants, as it's difficult to prevent them from being mixed into the soil during planting and maintenance.

In permanent plantings, apply a layer of mulch, 8 cm (3 in.) deep, around established plants. Wood chips are an excellent mulch material for your permanent garden. Spread the mulch on top of the soil, around the plants, but do not work it into the soil, where it can tie up nitrogen near plant roots. Decomposition at the soil surface does not usually cause problems with nitrogen availability. Apply mulch at least out to the drip line or outside edge of fruit trees and fruiting shrubs, or establish woody plants in a bed, and mulch the entire bed. Keep a 15 cm (6 in.) radius around the trunks of trees and shrubs clear of mulch, to discourage rodents that can damage the bark. When planting a fruit tree in a lawn, keep the area under the drip line free of grass, and mulch it instead. Taper the mulch depth so it is shallower near the crown of perennial plants, and allow a 5 cm (2 in.) ring around the crown that is mulch-free. Use discretion around groundcovers or young seedlings, and reduce the thickness of the layer if necessary.

The mulch in your permanent garden should be kept in place throughout the year, and topped up annually to maintain a depth of 8 cm (3 in.).

Starting Seeds Indoors

The temperature at which cool-season and warm-season crops germinate overlaps near 21°C (70°F), which makes it possible to start seeds indoors. The following suggestions will help you create a suitable environment to raise seedlings.

Containers: Seed-starting containers must be clean, deep enough for root growth, and have drainage holes. Compressed peat pots are popular, but they don't always decompose sufficiently for the roots to penetrate beyond the pots. If you use peat pots or pellets, thoroughly wet them before planting outdoors and install them so the top edge of each pot is below the soil surface; otherwise the protruding edge acts as a wick to draw moisture out from the area around your transplant.

Potting Mix: Garden soil is not recommended for indoor germination because it can contain weed seeds or disease organisms that thrive indoors and are detrimental to plants. Use a sterile, soil-less commercial potting mix or make up your own, using equal parts of horticultural vermiculite, perlite, and peat moss. Vermiculite and peat moss retain and exchange moisture and nutrients well, while perlite provides aeration and drainage. All three ingredients are free of disease and weed seeds, but they do not contain nutrients. These ingredients contain potentially harmful dust; you should wear a dust mask and thoroughly moisten them before handling them.

Coir has been introduced as a peat substitute for potting mixes because of environmental concerns over peat harvesting. Made up of coconut husk fibres, it's recycled waste from coconut processing. Coir is compressed into lightweight, dry bricks, which swell tremendously when wet. It's much easier to re-wet than peat and can be substituted directly for peat in a mix. Salt is sometimes used to process coir; obtain low-salt coir from a reputable source to avoid damaging your plants. Coir does

Warm-season basil benefits from a head start indoors.

Harvest earlier spring lettuce from seedlings germinated indoors.

not come without an environmental cost; it must be transported from the tropical areas where it is produced.

Sowing Seeds: Wet the planting mix thoroughly, then sow your seeds according to instructions on the seed packet. Label each container with the type of seed and planting date.

Thin crowded seedlings by snipping their stems off at soil level. Thick stands are susceptible to damping-off, a fungal disease that causes the irreversible collapse of seedlings. It occurs indoors when seedlings touch each other or are over-watered.

Water: After seeding, create a humid environment by covering the containers with clear plastic, supported by a wooden stake, or a rigid clear plastic dome. Remove the cover as soon as seeds sprout, and keep the soil moist like a damp sponge.

Temperature: Cool-season plants germinate at room temperature, but warm-season plants sprout faster when the soil is warmed by a heat source underneath the container. This is known as bottom heat, and there are commercially available devices for this purpose. The planted container can also be warmed near a furnace register or in a sunny window. As soon as the seedlings emerge, remove them from the heat source. Grow all seedlings under fluorescent lights in a cool room.

Light: Bright light is essential to prevent your seedlings from becoming spindly. They also need a cycle of alternating light and darkness to grow properly. Fluorescent lights provide the right spectrum of light for plant growth. Use grow lights, or one cool white and one warm white tube in a double fixture, and attach a timer to the fixture so that it provides fourteen to sixteen hours of light each day. The seedlings should be placed 8 cm (3 in.) below the light source at all stages of growth. It's a good idea to devise a system where either the plants or the lights can be moved to maintain this distance as the plants grow.

Fertilizer: Since the soil-less mix does not contain nutrients, it's necessary to incorporate a slow-release fertilizer in the planting mix before sowing seeds, or to fertilize every third irrigation as sprouts emerge, using a water-soluble houseplant fertilizer at the rate recommended on the package. Seeds do not require fertilizer until they sprout.

Transplanting Seedlings: Most garden seedlings produce a pair of seed leaves, called cotyledons, as they germinate. These first leaves look different than the true leaves that unfold above them. Exceptions include plants such as corn and onion, which send up a single leaf upon germination. When the first pair of true leaves appears, the seedlings should be transplanted. At this stage, seedlings that were started directly in individual containers, such as squash, can be transplanted into the garden if outdoor conditions are appropriate. Other seedlings should be transferred to individual containers that are at least 7.5 cm (3 in.) deep, and grown indoors until outdoor conditions are appropriate, or the roots fill the container and they require a larger pot.

Tomatoes must be started indoors or purchased as seedlings.

Pre-germination treatment of perennial herb seeds: The seeds of perennial plants survive winter in a dormant state and require signs of spring before they germinate. In nature, this requirement prevents them from germinating at the wrong time. It's possible to mimic spring conditions of melting snow with a process called moist-chilling or cool, moist stratification, by refrigerating the seeds in damp sand or vermiculite before planting them. Simply putting a seed packet in the freezer or refrigerator may not be adequate to break dormancy.

Mix your seeds with a handful of moist sterile sand or vermiculite. The mixture should be moist, but not soggy, to allow air exchange. Loosely seal the mixture in a plastic bag, allowing some air to remain in the bag. Label the mix and refrigerate it.

Refrigerate perennial herb seeds in moist vermiculite before sowing.

Most perennial species germinate faster after six weeks of moist-chilling. Schedule your treatment so the seeds are ready to plant at the right time; perennial herbs should be sown indoors about eight weeks before the frost date. If seeds sprout during moist-chilling, remove them from the refrigerator and plant them immediately.

Dividing Perennial Edibles

The easiest way to obtain more perennial edibles for your permanent garden is to divide existing plants. It involves digging up the desirable plant and separating it into two or more parts, which are then transplanted. Plants that grow from a taproot cannot be divided.

It's best to divide perennials when air temperatures are cool. Cool-season plants can be divided as new shoots emerge in early spring, or in September, when the soil is still warm. The ideal time to divide warm-season plants is in spring, as the new shoots appear at the soil surface. Some warm-season plants emerge quite late; it's easier to locate them if they are marked with a stake the previous fall. When dividing plants in autumn, do it at least six weeks before the ground freezes to allow root systems to establish before winter.

Choose a cool, cloudy evening and prepare the planting area first, so the divisions can be replanted immediately. Dig a hole large enough to accommodate the root ball, and slightly wider, and form a mound of soil in the centre.

Dig around the outside edge of the desired plant, lift it and pry it apart; minimize damage to the roots so that the plant recovers and becomes re-established quickly. A knife might be required to separate plants with thick root balls, or suckers, such as raspberries.

Each division should be replanted at the same depth as the original plant. Place the new transplant on the mound, with the crown of the plant where the stem meets the roots at soil level, spreading the roots out in a radial fashion over the mound. Backfill the planting hole, and create a shallow irrigation basin around the plant, out to the edge of the leaves and roots, then firm the soil around it.

Thoroughly water each division by filling the basin with water immediately after transplanting, and apply mulch, tapering the depth of the mulch so it becomes shallow toward the crown of the plant, and leave a ring around the crown that is mulch-free.

Monitor the plant for signs of wilt and keep the soil moist for at least six weeks, or until new growth indicates that the plant has established roots. The aboveground portion of plant divisions made in autumn will freeze back; leave the spent stems in place until the following spring when new shoots show that the plant rooted and survived winter successfully.

A 'Honey Red' rhubarb division rapidly grows into a large plant.

CHAPTER THREE

Growing and Harvesting the Edible Garden

Watering Edible Plants

Edible plants need ample water, and it should be applied deeply to encourage strong, extensive roots, allowing the soil to become slightly dry between irrigations. Weather conditions, soil texture, and the type of plant will influence how often you need to water.

Keep the soil consistently moist in your seasonal garden as your seeds germinate and when you set out transplants. When young seedlings and transplants put on new growth, switch to giving them a weekly soak. Established annual vegetables and herbs need about 2.5 cm (1 in.) of water in a single precipitation or irrigation event each week during the growing season. During hot, windy weather, it may be necessary to water more often to prevent stress and wilting. Late in the season, water should be withheld from some vegetable crops, such as garlic, onions, and potatoes to ready them for harvest.

Fruit trees, fruiting shrubs, and perennial edibles in your permanent garden require regular deep irrigation during the first three years as they become established. Irrigate them approximately twice a week during the first month after planting, and once a week for the remainder of the season. Slowly fill a shallow basin around each plant, out to the edge of the plant canopy, so that water moves throughout and just beyond the roots. Continue to monitor the soil weekly during the second and third season after planting, and water approximately every week to two weeks. As fruit trees and fruiting shrubs begin bearing, irrigate them deeply during flowering and fruit formation in June and early July.

Withhold water from fruit trees and fruiting shrubs in late summer to help them harden off.

Rain barrels conserve water by collecting precipitation for supplemental irrigation.

A soaker hose applies water efficiently at the base of plants.

Withhold water from your fruit trees and fruiting shrubs as the summer heat fades in August to slow their growth, so that they can harden off and enter a dormant state for winter. The hardening off process occurs as autumn temperatures drop and days grow shorter, but it doesn't take place if the plants are still actively growing. After the leaves drop, but before the ground freezes, irrigate them deeply in late autumn. The final fall irrigation is especially important in Chinook areas to prevent winter desiccation.

Water is a precious resource that should be used wisely. It's best to irrigate in the morning, when evaporation caused by sun and wind is low, and to apply water slowly so that it seeps into the soil. The most efficient way to deliver water to edible plants is through a soaker hose or drip system.

Coordinate your irrigations with natural precipitation using a rain gauge, and water soon after the rain stops to reach the quota that your plants need. The rainfall that runs off your roof can be collected for use during drier times in rain barrels at the base of your downspouts.

Fertilizing Edible Plants

Plants obtain their nutrients from minerals in the soil. Large amounts of nitrogen, phosphorous, and potassium are required; these are known as macronutrients and are the major components of natural and synthetic fertilizers. Nitrogen is usually the nutrient that limits plant growth because it's often in short supply. Plants also need relatively large quantities of calcium, sulphur, and magnesium. The remaining minerals, called micronutrients, are needed in small quantities; these include boron, chlorine, copper, iron, manganese, molybdenum, and zinc.

If a nutrient is in a form that plants can use, the plant doesn't distinguish whether it came from a synthetic or natural source. However, the source does make a difference to the soil and the creatures that dwell there. Compost is a natural source that also supplies organic matter, which supports beneficial soil life and helps retain nutrients and make them more readily available to plant roots. Since compost comes from plants that previously took up minerals, it is a complete fertilizer that contains small quantities of all essential nutrients, including micronutrients, although its composition depends on the raw materials that produced it. The nutrients are slowly released as the compost decomposes, similar to what occurs in nature.

Synthetic fertilizers contain known concentrations of specific minerals in the correct useable form for plants. They are soluble in water, and are useful to deliver nutrients and correct particular deficiencies quickly; they can also be manufactured in a slow-release form, which dissolves and releases nutrients over time. Synthetic fertilizers are manmade and don't add organic matter to the soil. The ingredients may not include micronutrients or all the macronutrients.

Other natural nutrient sources such as bonemeal, blood meal, seaweed extracts, and fish emulsions contain small amounts of certain minerals that are slowly released through the activity of microorganisms. These supplements are useful when there is a need for a particular nutrient, such as nitrogen, that has been shown on an ongoing basis. These sources release nutrients too slowly to be effective at correcting a pressing deficiency.

Fertilizer labels for nutrients that originate from natural or synthetic sources indicate the ratio of nitrogen (N), phosphorus (P) and potassium (K) to each

Soil nutrients must be replenished after this productive garden of beans, beets, carrots, tomatoes, broad beans, and potatoes is harvested.

other, expressed as three numbers (N-P-K), always in that order; a zero indicates the mineral is not included.

When crops are harvested, it's necessary to replace the nutrients those plants used, or the soil will become depleted. However, it's important to apply only what is necessary, because too much fertilizer can cause problems. Excess nitrogen promotes leafy stems at the expense of flowers and fruits, and it can burn foliage. Lush growth is also prone to drought, insect, and disease problems, and it's slow to harden off for winter. Contrary to popular opinion, studies have shown that high phosphorous fertilizers, such as bonemeal, do not increase rooting or flowering unless the soil is deficient; in fact, excess phosphorous can disrupt the beneficial fungi that attach to plant roots and help them obtain nutrients. As a result, the plants have to work harder to get the nutrients.

Fertilizing practices affect environments far beyond your garden. Nitrogen from both natural and synthetic sources can be swept away by run-off into storm sewers, eventually polluting rivers and lakes, and the influx causes algae to grow out of control, which negatively affects fish and other life. Environmental costs also result from fertilizer production. The high temperature and

Pale young plum leaves with dark green veins indicate that iron may be unavailable to the plant.

pressure necessary to produce synthetic nitrogen fertilizer requires energy that usually comes from fossil fuels, and mined phosphorous and potassium are also non-renewable resources.

Supplying Nutrients in the Garden: Unless a specific nutrient need has been identified through a soil test, a simple, environmentally sound way to replenish your soil and nourish your plants is to apply compost and mulch.

Your seasonal vegetable garden needs to be replenished with nutrients every year, particularly with nitrogen. Use high quality compost that has matured at least six months or purchase Type A compost, and spread a 1 cm (0.5 in.) layer across the planting area in spring and again in late June. Compost can be used in the same manner to feed your outdoor container plants.

Woody fruits and perennials usually grow satisfactorily in prairie soils without supplements when a layer of mulch is maintained around them, as nutrients are released during decomposition. If a soil test or plant deficiency indicates that fertilizer is necessary, apply it in small amounts in spring. Never fertilize woody fruits after the end of June, as it stimulates growth that doesn't have time to harden off properly before winter. Current research shows that you should not fertilize young fruit trees, because it promotes vegetative growth and causes the plant to take longer to mature and fruit. Tender growth on fruit trees is also very susceptible to a disease known as fire blight.

If your plants look healthy, they are probably getting what they need. Poor plant growth or pale foliage may indicate that nutrients are lacking, but similar symptoms are caused by too much or too little water, disease, injury, herbicide damage, or a problem with soil texture or pH. For example, alkaline soils can make iron and manganese unavailable to plants, causing yellowing of the leaves, even though the minerals are present in the soil. To treat symptoms correctly, it's important to have background information about your soil in order to identify the true cause.

COMPOST TEA

Compost tea, made by brewing compost in a bucket of water, potentially contains harmful bacteria, since it is difficult to regulate its production. Specialized equipment that uses additives or aerators can increase this risk, and compost tea made with this equipment is not recommended for use on food crops. It's easier and safer to apply compost directly on your garden, where it benefits the soil in addition to supplying nutrients.

Weeds

Weeds should be removed promptly and sent to the compost pile, because they compete with your plants for sun, moisture, and nutrients. Hand pulling is the best way to eliminate undesirable plants; avoid using chemical herbicides, especially where you grow food.

THINNING SEEDLINGS

In the seasonal garden, it's necessary to remove seedlings of desirable plants when they sprout too close together, as they compete with each other for light, moisture, and nutrients, just like weeds do. Thin seedlings when they reach 2.5 to 5 cm (1 to 2 in.) tall so that they are spaced 5 cm (2 in.) apart. Thin the plants in stages as their leaves grow enough to touch each other, until each plant has the recommended amount of space around it. Thinned salad plant seedlings are edible and can be tossed with other baby greens.

Sunlight promotes weed seed germination, and the two best ways to prevent weed seeds from getting the light they need are to cover the soil with mulch, and to avoid turning the soil, which brings seeds to the surface. In addition, space your desirable plants so that the foliage of mature plants shades the soil and outcompetes the weeds.

Try to remove weeds before they produce seeds, and unearth the entire root system to prevent re-sprouting. Perennial weeds can be tenacious, especially if they re-grow from pieces of root. Persistent eradication of new sprouts will eventually deplete food reserves in the roots, causing the unwanted plants to die. Lift invasive roots with a digging fork and tease them out of the soil without breaking them, because chopped roots multiply into more weeds.

Pruning Woody Fruits

The goal of most pruning is to highlight and maintain the natural shape of the plant, and to remove dead, damaged or diseased branches. Fruiting plants are also pruned to make them more productive, easier to harvest, and as a means of controlling some disease problems.

It's important to prune at the right time of year, and most (but not all)

Remove weeds and thin seedlings so plants are spaced properly.

woody plants on the prairies should be pruned in early spring, usually in late March, after the coldest part of winter has passed, but while the plants are still dormant. At this time, plants heal quickly from pruning cuts and it is easier to see their form when there are no leaves. Plants that should be pruned later in spring include those that are grown for their flowers, like lilacs, those that bleed sap profusely in early spring like maples and birches, and fruits. In colder zones of the prairies, it's recommended that you prune fruit trees and fruiting shrubs just as the buds noticeably swell, but before they break open, usually in late April. The swollen buds will demonstrate whether the branches survived winter.

Pruning stimulates growth, so it's important not to do major pruning after the end of June, to avoid promoting growth that doesn't have time to harden off for winter. However, dead, damaged, or diseased branches should always be removed as soon as you notice them. Any suckers that sprout near the base of the plant should also be removed when they appear.

Keep pruning tools sharp; clean dirt and debris from the pruning blade and prevent pitting and rust by wiping it with an oily cloth. When removing diseased branches, wipe your tool after each cut with a household disinfectant such as Lysol or rubbing alcohol to avoid spreading the disease.

Fruit Trees: Young fruit trees should be pruned to build a strong structure that can support a heavy crop. Choose one branch to be the central leader, and remove branches that compete with it. Below the leader, aim to have four to six lateral branches that radiate in all directions, and are spaced evenly along the trunk, about 30 cm (12 in.) apart, with the lowest branch at least

60 cm (2 ft.) above the ground. If there are not enough lateral branches to choose from, remove the top third of the current season's growth from the leader to encourage the side buds to sprout new laterals.

Remove branches that form narrow angles with the trunk, and select branches that are closer to horizontal than vertical. A branch that meets the trunk at a wide angle is stronger than one at a narrow angle, and will bear the weight of fruit better. Limit pruning on young trees to the selection of these main branches and removing dead, damaged, and diseased wood.

Once the tree reaches fruit-bearing age, maintain it with moderate yearly pruning. Remove less than one-fourth of the wood each year; heavy pruning stimulates a proliferation of weak growth. Examine the entire tree before pruning and remove:

Train young fruit trees to have a central leader with six lateral branches radiating out from it.

1. Branches that cross or rub on each other
2. Branches that grow in toward the centre of the tree
3. Branches that compete for the same space
4. Water sprouts that grow straight up from a branch
5. Suckers that sprout from the base of the trunk

Two types of cuts are made to maintain the size and shape of a mature tree. "Thinning" cuts remove an entire stem or branch back to where it originates at another branch or the trunk. Thinning improves sunlight and air circulation within the tree canopy. "Heading back" cuts control tree size, by removing part of the previous year's growth to a point that is just above an outward-facing bud. That bud will sprout in the direction it is facing on the branch. Don't leave

Heading back cuts remove part of the previous year's growth.

Thinning cuts remove an entire branch from where it originates.

stubs on the tree after thinning or heading back cuts. Use a pruning shears to re-move stems less than 1 cm (0.5 in.) in diameter, and use loppers to cut branches up to 3.5 cm (1.5 in.).

Remove large branches at the collar, where the branch joins another branch or the trunk. The collar contains healing properties, and it appears as a slight swelling or a few wrinkles where the two branches meet. Make a clean cut just outside the collar, at an angle that matches its shape. Don't seal the cut with pruning paint; it interferes with the tree's natural disease barrier at that location.

To remove large branches without damaging your tree, use a pruning saw and make a series of three cuts. The first cut should be made on the underside of the limb about 15 to 30 cm (6 to 12 in.) out from the trunk, cutting upwards into the bottom half of the branch. The second cut is made just beyond the first cut, from the top, downwards through the branch, removing it. The third cut removes the stump, and is made just outside the collar where the branch meets the trunk, following the angle of the collar.

Prune a mature tree by thinning the outer branches, removing those that overlap or are close together. To control size, head back some of the previous year's growth. If necessary, the height can be reduced by pruning the leader back to a desirable lateral branch, but never indiscriminately chop the top off.

Fruiting Shrubs: Fruiting shrubs should be lightly pruned each year to main-tain productivity and to prevent them from becoming overgrown. Remove

Keep fruiting shrubs productive by annual pruning before they break bud.

ESPALIER

· · · · · · · · · · · ·

Intricate pruning styles such as espalier have been developed to grow fruit, such as apples, in small growing spaces. Commitment is required to train a three-dimensional plant to grow in a two-dimensional space, as the tree must be pruned and tied in place every spring. A simple, classic pattern of espalier is described here; there are many others.

Choose a young tree and plant it close to a sturdy trellis with horizontal wires to train the branches on. The trellis can be adjacent to a wall or fence, with space for air circulation in between, or it can be constructed so it is free-standing in a bed.

In early spring, as the buds swell but before they break, cut the tree back to 45 to 60 cm (18 to 24 in.) above the ground, keeping three swollen buds below the cut. As the buds sprout, gently bend and spread the two lower shoots in opposite directions and tie them loosely to the trellis, so they extend horizontally from a forty-five degree angle at the main trunk. Allow the third bud to grow straight up and become the leader. In early June, pinch back the side shoots that develop along the two horizontal branches, so that each side shoot has only two or three leaves.

The following spring, before the buds break, head back the central vertical leader to three good swollen buds, spaced 30 to 45 cm (12 to 18 in.) above the first set of horizontal branches. Again, spread and tie two of the new sprouts so that they are somewhat horizontal, at a forty-five degree angle to the trunk, while allowing the third to grow straight up. Continue to repeat this process each year until the plant reaches the desired height, and maintain it by annual pinching and pruning.

Espalier is a technique where fruits are pruned and tied to grow in a two-dimensional space.

about one-fifth of the plant each year; keep the younger branches to bear fruit and prune out older branches all the way back to the soil line near the base of the plant. This rejuvenates the shrub and opens up the plant to receive better light penetration and air circulation.

Pollination and Fruiting

Many plants require cross-pollination be-tween two different cultivars of the same spe-cies, where pollen is carried from one plant to another by insects in order to produce fruit. Apples, crabapples, pears and plums need to receive pollen from a different, but com-patible cultivar, called a pollinizer, with an overlapping bloom period. In urban neigh-bourhoods, there is often a suitable variety

Pear blossoms need pollen from a different pear cultivar to produce fruit.

within range. Plants like the sour cherry are self-fruitful and don't need cross-pollination, but may set more fruit if another cultivar is close by.

Other conditions need to be met to produce fruit, and a lack of fruit may occur during these circumstances:

1. There is no appropriate cultivar nearby for cross-pollination.
2. Spring conditions such as cool temperatures, wind, or rain may have hindered pollinating insects.
3. Flower buds were killed by a freeze after dormancy was broken.
4. Blossoms were injured by frost.
5. The cultivar has an alternate bearing habit and produces fruit every second year.
6. The plant has been affected by disease.
7. Adverse conditions were present when flower buds formed the previous summer.

Apples should be thinned to increase fruit size and quality.

Thinning Fruit

After pollination, fruit trees that become too heavily laden with developing fruits shed some of their load. This natural drop usually occurs twice: a couple weeks after the petals fall, and again in June. It's advisable to thin the load further to increase the size and quality of the remaining fruit. Thinning reduces the stress of heavy production and decreases the potential for broken limbs or a small crop the following year. Apples, pears, and plums should be thinned, but smaller fruits are not usually thinned.

Thinning is accomplished by removing blossoms or fruit; most gardeners find it less tedious to thin small fruits in June. Remove all the fruits from each cluster, except the best blemish-free one, taking care not to damage the spur it is attached to. Allow 20 to 25 cm (8 to 10 in.) between apples and pears, and thin plums 10 to 15 cm (4 to 6 in.) apart, or thin so that the distance between fruits is at least the width of your hand.

Pest and Disease Prevention

Your best defence against plant pests and diseases is to choose resistant cultivars, to produce robust plants with good gardening practices, to keep your garden

A diverse planting of herbs and edible flowers attracts natural predators and pollinators.

clean by removing fallen fruit and diseased and spent plant parts, and to have a diverse planting that attracts a variety of natural predators and pollinators. Many insects, bacteria, and fungi are beneficial and will help you keep pest and disease problems in check. In addition, a few simple measures can prevent some pests from ever becoming problems.

SUNSCALD

Fruit trees can be damaged by sunscald on the southwest side of the trunk, caused by freeze-thaw cycles in late winter or early spring. Direct sun combined with reflected light off the snow thaws plant tissues during the day, and they freeze when temperatures plunge at night. Protect your trees from sunscald by installing tree wrap or tree guards, coating the trunk with white latex paint, or planting an evergreen shrub such that it casts shade on the southwest side of the trunk. Trees on northern exposures are less likely to be affected.

Avoid using pesticides in your edible garden; if you spray anything, be absolutely sure that it's food-safe and intended for your particular plant and problem. Pesticide labels are required by law for your own protection, and should be followed exactly. Those that are labelled "organic" may be derived from natural sources, but that doesn't guarantee safety, and some are toxic to animals, insects, or fish. Pesticides from natural or man-made sources that are non-specific will harm beneficial insects as well as the target. Home remedies aren't necessarily safer or effective, and concoctions such as ordinary dish soap and water can actually burn your plants.

Along with good cultivation practices, a hose can help rid your plants of some pests. A strong blast works well to dislodge aphids from infested plants, and the moisture discourages spider mites in hot, dry weather. Whenever you wet the leaves, allow time for them to dry before evening to avoid problems with powdery mildew.

Handpicking of some insects is effective, especially in the initial stages. Traps are also useful to collect certain pests; slugs are easily lured under a damp board and aphids can be trapped on yellow sticky cards mounted among your plants.

Reduce problems by rotating crops in your seasonal garden each year.

Physical barriers such as a 1.8 to 2.4 m (6 to 8 ft.) fence can hinder unin-vited pets and deer, and 90 cm (3 ft.) high wire mesh might stop rabbits from wreaking havoc. To block burrowing creatures, bend the bottom of the fence out at an angle and bury it several inches deep. Prevent mice from chewing on the bark of trees during winter by wrapping the base of the tree with wire mesh in autumn, or applying tree guards, which also protect the tree from sunscald. Bird netting is the best barrier to keep birds from taking your share of fruit. Raise the netting off the plants if possible, because some birds will use it as a perch while they dodge their beaks between the openings and feast on the fruits.

Pest and Disease Prevention in the Seasonal Garden

Crop rotation: The purpose of crop rotation is to change your yearly garden layout in order to prevent a build-up of pests that might overwinter in the soil, and to prevent certain nutrients from becoming depleted in one spot. Keep a simple diagram that shows the layout of your seasonal garden, and make sure that members of the same family are not grown in the same place for at least three consecutive years. For example, tomatoes, peppers, and potatoes are re-

Floating row covers can prevent damage from pests like these flea beetles on kale.

lated and share similar pests and diseases, so these plants should be moved to a different bed each year, or to a different location in the same bed.

Physical barriers: Floating row covers can prevent insects or their larvae from feeding on your plants. The cover should be applied early in the season, allowing room for growth, and sealed around the edges with soil, and must be removed during flowering, unless you hand-pollinate the crop.

Diatomaceous earth is an abrasive powder made up of tiny fossilized marine creatures that can be sprinkled around the base of seasonal plants. It desiccates the bodies of soft-bellied pests, such as slugs as they crawl over it. It is easily washed away, and needs to be reapplied after a rain or irrigation. Boric acid is an alternate material that is used in the same way.

Protect young transplants from cutworms, which chew seedlings off at the soil line, by slipping a cardboard collar around the individual stems as they are transplanted. The collar should extend 5 cm (2 in.) above and 2.5 cm (1 in.) below the soil. A pencil or a nail stuck into the soil right next to the stem can also prevent the cutworm from chewing around it.

Disease Control in the Permanent Garden

If caught early, certain diseases that affect woody fruits can be controlled with pruning.

Fire blight: Fire blight is a bacterial disease that affects plants in the rose family, including apples, crabapples, pears, and saskatoons. It's spread by pollinating insects, rain, wind, and pruning tools. Infected blossoms turn brown, and tips of leafy branches become crispy and curl at the tip. The plant looks scorched and bacterial slime may

Fireblight on apple can be controlled by removing affected branches.

ooze from infected spots. Remove infected branches immediately, 30 cm (12 in.) below the site of infection, and burn or dispose of them.

Black knot: Black knot is a fungus that affects chokecherry, plum, and cherry relatives. The fungal spores are carried by wind or rain from infected to healthy branches in spring. Swellings appear at the infected site and enlarge into hard, black masses the following spring. Remove infected branches 30 cm (12 in.) below the infection site and dispose of them.

Juniper/saskatoon rust: This fungal disease requires two hosts; its primary host is the juniper, where it forms brown galls that sprout gelatinous, orange spore-horns after a rainy period in spring. The spores infect a secondary host in the rose family, usually saskatoon, causing small orange spots to appear on the upper leaf surface and berries. These spots produce spores that are carried back to the primary juniper host. The fungus requires both hosts to survive, and spores can be transported by wind over long distances. Remove juniper branches that display galls, and dispose of fallen saskatoon leaves and berries in autumn.

Gathering the Harvest

The harvest is the most anticipated part of the season, and these suggestions will help you enjoy your produce at its peak flavour. Specific instructions for harvesting each crop are included with every individual plant description.

Vegetables and Fruits: Harvest vegetables and fruits before mid-morning, when they are crisp and temperatures are cool, or just before preparing them for a meal.

Salad greens are harvested by cutting off mature heads, picking leaves from the outer edges of the plant, or using the "cut-and-come-again" method. The latter method involves slicing off the entire leaf clump with a sharp knife, when the foliage is 5 to 10 cm (2 to 4 in.) long, leaving a 2.5 cm (1 in.) stem above ground to sprout another clump; it works well for two or three cuts and then the leaves become tough. Rinse all salad greens immediately after harvest and pat them dry or dry them in a salad spinner. Refrigerate them in a container or a perforated plastic bag that is intended for produce to maintain humidity and keep the greens crisp.

Harvest fruits, including peppers, tomatoes, and squash, with the stems attached. Fruits and root vegetables keep better unwashed. Remove the tops from root vegetables, and brush the dirt off them before storing. Refrigerate most vegetables in perforated plastic produce bags or enclose them in a plastic bag with a damp cloth. Refrigerate fragile fruits, like berries, in hard-sided containers that are covered. Tomatoes, melons, and pears should be stored at room temperature for optimum flavour, and potatoes, winter squash, dry onions, and garlic should be stored in a cool, dark place, but not refrigerated.

Before freezing vegetables, it's best to preserve their colour and texture by blanching, which stops the enzyme action that causes them to deteriorate. Blanching is done by briefly plunging the vegetable in boiling water, followed by immediate cooling in ice water.

A completely different procedure that is also called blanching is done in the garden with some vegetables, such as endive and leeks, just before harvest. This process blocks sunlight from the edible portion of the plant, so that the edible part becomes pale and tastes milder.

Newly harvested 'Yukon Gold' potatoes

Ripe 'Prairie Magic' apples PHOTO - JEFFRIES NURSERY   Harvest herbs just before using them to retain peak quality.

Previous generations preserved vegetables by canning, pickling, or storing them in root cellars. Contemporary gardeners have devised storage areas to keep winter squash, onions, and potatoes in cool, dark basements or wine cellars. A makeshift root cellar can be made by digging an outdoor pit 1 m (1 yd.) deep, to stow alternating layers of carrots with slightly damp soil, covered with 30 cm (12 in.) of insulating material and a waterproof tarp, or by simply leaving hardy root vegetables such as parsnips or carrots in the ground, covered by bales of straw to insulate them.

Herbs: For peak quality, harvest herbs just before using them. Rinse the foliage to remove soil and insects, pat or spin them dry immediately to prevent the leaves from getting water-soaked, and store it in the refrigerator. Chop the leaves to release their fragrant oils, or keep herb leaves intact on their stems to flavour the dish, and remove the entire stem before serving. An occasional snip is fine anytime, but to help your perennial herbs survive winter, stop harvesting them heavily six weeks before the expected autumn frost date.

Freezing Herbs: Most herbs retain good flavour when they are frozen. Freeze herbs with pliable stems, like dill, with the leaves attached to stems. Herbs with large leaves such as basil and Italian parsley should be blanched before freezing. Remove leaves from thick or woody stems, like those of tarragon, and chop them before packing them in airtight freezer bags.

Drying Herbs: Drying concentrates the flavour and increases pungency of some herbs. Tie the stems in bunches with an elastic band and hang the bunches up-side down in a dark, well-ventilated place, or spread clean leaves or sprigs on a screen or paper towel, and dry them until the leaves feel crisp and brittle, for about two weeks. After drying, strip the leaves from the stems and store them in a tightly sealed glass jar, away from light.

Finely crumble your dried herbs just before using them. When substituting dried herbs in place of fresh ones in a recipe, use one-third to one-half the amount.

Saving Seeds

Saving Pure Seeds: Self-pollinated plants have the ability to set seeds without receiving pollen from another plant, although their flowers can be visited by insects. Seeds from self-pollinated plants, like beans, peas, lettuce, tomatoes, chicory, and endive, are likely to remain fairly pure and produce plants with similar characteristics in the next generation.

Most edible plants are cross-pollinated by insects or wind; one plant needs to receive pollen from another plant of the same species to set seeds. It's difficult to save pure strains of seeds from wind-pollinated plants, because the pollen is so light it can drift 1.6 km (1 mile). Plants that are cross-pollinated by insects might receive pollen from a nearby garden, as insects indiscriminately move around within 0.4 km (0.25 mile). To produce seeds that are pure, cross-pollinated cultivars must be isolated from different cultivars of the same species, and the most practical way to do this is to install a barrier.

Two types of barriers are commonly used to collect pure seeds of cross-pollinated plants. A lightweight floating row cover can be installed over the plants and sealed at the edges with soil, or individual flower buds on different plants can be enclosed in small bags. The bags should made from tightly woven

Dill seeds are ready to collect.

Lettuce is allowed to bloom and set seed for collection.

The swelling at the base of the female 'Buttercup' squash flower (on the left) distinguishes it from the male flower.

In order to collect pure squash seeds, insects must be prevented from cross-pollinating the blossoms.

material that allows light and air to pass through, such as pieces of nylon stocking or floating row cover. The barriers should be installed before plants bloom, and you will need to hand-pollinate to obtain fruits and seeds.

Bagging is usually done on large flowers, such as squash. Squash plants have separate male and female flowers, so it's necessary to choose male and female flower buds on different plants; the females can be distinguished by swellings that resemble miniature fruit below the petals. Enclose each selected bud in a separate bag and tie the bag shut, using cotton balls between the stem and the bag to cushion the stem, so the tie doesn't constrict it.

Hand-Pollinating Plants: Pollination is done by transferring pollen from the male anthers in the centre of one flower, to the sticky female stigma in the centre of a flower on a different plant. A fine paintbrush is usually the best tool to transfer pollen, by dabbing it inside large flowers such as squash or by brushing it across the heads of multiple tiny flowers like those of dill. Use a botany book to identify flower parts, as they differ among the plant families. Hand-pollination is also used to improve yields.

It's not necessary to isolate plants during pollination if you are simply trying to increase yields, but some kind of barrier is necessary if your pollination purpose is to collect pure seeds. Remove the barrier while you hand-pollinate,

'Sunburst' patty-pan squash with flower buds and developing fruits.

and replace it immediately after to prevent potential contamination from insects. On plants, such as squash, where flowers are individually bagged, keep the female flower enclosed until the fruit swells and shows signs of developing; then the bag can be removed to allow room for growth.

Saving Seeds from Biennials: It's easiest to collect seeds from annual plants at the end of the season. Biennials present another challenge: getting them through winter. Hardier species like chard, chicory, parsley, parsnips, shallots, leeks, and even carrots may survive if they are covered with insulating mulch until early spring. Otherwise, the roots must be dug and overwintered using these guidelines:

1. Choose twelve healthy plants for storage; avoid those that bolt.
2. Lift the roots, leaving a 2.5 cm (1 in.) top attached above the crown, and dry the skin indoors for 1 to 2 days, but don't let the root go limp.
3. Store roots in damp sand in a cool place where they won't freeze, or refrigerated in a perforated plastic bag.
4. Inspect roots for rot and plant them outdoors when the soil can be worked in spring, after the danger of heavy frost is over.

Collecting seeds: Choose and mark at least five healthy plants of the same cultivar. Observe seed heads or fruits closely, and collect them when they are completely ripe, and have dried or changed colour. Harvest pods or stalks just before they dry or enclose them in a paper or cloth bag to catch seeds if they shatter. Moist fruits should be left on the vine past the prime edible stage, until their seeds mature and change from green to white, brown, or black.

If you continue the cycle of collecting and growing out seeds from your plants each year,

Biennial leeks bloom and set seed the second year after planting.

it's possible to develop a strain that is particularly suited to conditions in your area. Collect seeds from as many plants as possible to preserve the strength, diversity, and versatility of your strain.

Cleaning, Drying, and Storing Seeds: Harvested seeds should be separated from other plant parts, such as pods, stalks, or fruit, and then dried at room temperature on paper or a screen for two weeks. Entire seed heads can be dried in paper bags before stripping the seeds from the stalks. Seeds of fleshy fruit should be cleaned from the fruit and rinsed before drying. Dry these on a non-absorbing surface such as a screen or a glass dish so they don't stick and chip when you try to remove them.

It's a good idea to ferment seeds of moist fruits, like tomato and cucumber, before drying them. Fermenting helps kill seed-borne bacteria that cause disease. A similar process occurs in nature when fruit ripens, falls to the ground, and rots. Reproduce this process by scooping tomato or cucumber seeds and some pulp into a glass container, and leave the mixture at room temperature for a couple days. In two to three days, add enough water to completely cover the fermenting (smelly) seeds; dead seeds float and the viable seeds will sink. Pour off the dead seeds and water, and rinse the viable seeds through a strainer.

Silica gel is a useful desiccant to completely dry seeds. Use equal amounts of silica gel and seeds, and place the seeds in an envelope before enclosing them in an airtight glass jar with silica gel. Allow one week for drying. The silica gel can be used repeatedly if it's dried in an oven or microwave between uses.

Package your dry seeds in a paper envelope, labelled with the cultivar name

Ferment freshly collected tomato seed to reduce seed-borne diseases.

and date of storage, and store the envelopes in airtight containers in a cool, dark, dry place.

Closing the Growing Season …

The first fall frost is the official close of the growing season. You may be able to extend the season by protecting your plants with blankets, and some crops are ready to harvest around this time, but the days of carefree cultivating are over.

After harvesting the summer bounty, autumn is the time to remove the remains of annual plants from your seasonal garden. This reduces over-wintering sites for insects and disease organisms. Disease-free plants can be composted, and will break down faster if they are shredded first.

Gather the fallen leaves from woody plants and perennials in your permanent garden, and add them to the compost pile. You can promote decomposition by chopping up plant stems and shredding leaves with a lawn mower. Shredded leaves can also be used as mulch in a location that is sheltered from strong winds. Let the spent stems of perennial plants remain standing to trap insulating mulch and snow during winter, and remove them the following spring once growth resumes.

In anticipation of the next season, turn over the soil in your seasonal planting area, and clean, lubricate, and store your gardening tools. Finish the season by planting garlic bulbs in early fall and sowing seeds of the hardiest cool-season plants in late October, after it is too chilly for them to germinate. When the soil warms up the following spring, these early sprouts could launch your next gardening season.

'Rescue' crabapples

CHAPTER **FOUR**

Edible Plants for the Seasonal Garden: Annual Vegetables and Herbs

In the seasonal garden, you can transform bare soil into a bountiful basket of fresh ingredients for salads, soups, and seasonings in a single growing season. Each year brings exciting promise and potential to create beauty and sustenance in your own backyard with the plants described in this chapter.

The plant profiles are divided into two groups and listed by common name in alphabetical order. The first group is made up of cool-season greens and roots that can be sown after snowmelt makes way for spring. The warm-season plants that announce summer are described in the second section.

Each description begins with a quick reference to help you plan and plant your seasonal garden. Use the plant spacing as a guideline for thinning seedlings, and note that the space between plants varies depending on what stage and which part of the plant you plan to use. The preferred amount of light each plant needs is listed first. The descriptions also outline when to sow seeds indoors or outdoors and indicate how long your seeds will remain viable. Particulars on how to grow, harvest, and collect seeds from each plant are designed to supplement the information in the first three chapters of this book. The ripening cues described for each crop are good harvest guidelines, but you should compare these with the seed package description of your particular cultivar. The plant profiles also present simple tips to help you prepare, enjoy, or preserve the peak flavour of your homegrown produce.

*... **For the Enthusiastic Gardener*** highlights particular plants that might require extra effort or growing space in order to successfully harvest a crop in some regions. Most need a long growing season or have persistent pest prob-

'Late Flat Dutch' cabbage

lems and suggestions for overcoming these challenges are provided with the plant profile.

The cultivar lists were compiled from personal experience and suggestions by prairie gardeners, and each has unique or worthwhile characteristics, a history, or a cultural link. Performance in the prairie climate, disease and insect resistance, exceptional yield, and unusual colours and shapes were also among the criteria used to decide which ones made the list. From tried and true heirlooms to new or popular hybrids, these cultivars were chosen because gardeners and growers are talking about them, growing them, and serving them on the table. All are commercially available, but finding some will be like a treasure hunt. The intent is to present you with an assortment of named selections that have delighted prairie gardeners, acknowledging that flavour ratings are a matter of personal preference.

The suggested cultivars represent a very limited cross-section of what can be grown in prairie gardens. Another source to find evaluations of new and old cultivars is the University of Saskatchewan's annual "Vegetable Cultivar and Cultural Trials," which is posted after each season on their Web site.

Many of the crops described *... **For the Enthusiastic Gardener*** require a large growing space.

'Ruby' chard

'Crosby's Egyptian' beet

'Detroit Red' beet greens

Cool-season Vegetables and Herbs
Beets and Chard

Beta vulgaris subsp. *vulgaris*
Family: goosefoot (*Chenopodiaceae*)
Type: cool-season biennial
Height: beets 25 cm (10 in.); chard 45 cm (18 in.)
Space: beets 5 to 7.5 cm (2 to 3 in.) for baby beets, 10 cm (4 in.) for full-size roots; chard 7.5 cm (3 in.) for baby greens, 20 cm (8 in.) for mature greens
Light: full sun to part shade
Propagation: seed outdoors in early to mid-May
Seed Viability: retains 50% germination for 6 years

Originally from the Mediterranean region, beets and chard are closely related plants of the same species. Chard varieties (also known as Swiss chard) were domesticated to favour luxuriant leaves, while beet varieties were chosen for large, sweet roots. Chard foliage was used medicinally and as a potherb before Greek and Roman times. Beets are a more recent development; the cultivation of plants with thickened roots was first recorded during the thirteenth century in Italy. Sugar beets were also developed from this species after the process to extract sugar from them was discovered in Europe in the 1700s.

Beets and chard are related to spinach and their greens are prepared and consumed similarly. Many gardeners prefer growing chard to spinach because it produces edible greens for a much longer season. Chard is frost and heat tolerant, and as a biennial, it doesn't bolt the first season like spinach does. In addition, chard is a gorgeous plant that grows well in containers.

Both chard and beets contain pigments that can produce intensely coloured roots and leaves that contrast beautifully with other vegetables and flowers. Chard leaves have a prominent mid rib that is vivid scarlet, yellow, orange, white, or purple. A cross-section of a beet reveals alternating rings of root tissue, referred to as "zoning," in shades of burgundy, yellow, or white. Golden beets lack the stain-producing pigments of red beets.

How to Grow: Beets and chard have similar growing requirements. Their so-called "seeds" are actually dry, pointed fruits that contain several seeds. It's difficult to separate the seeds before planting, so they must be thinned after they sprout in a clump. The seeds contain a germination inhibitor that can be removed with water. Soak the seeds for one to two hours, or roll them up in a damp paper towel overnight before sowing them.

Sow beet and chard seeds outdoors, 1 cm (0.5 in.) deep and 2.5 cm (1 in.) apart, two to three weeks before the frost date. Plant them in soil that is loose to a depth of at least 20 cm (8 in.). Additional sowings can be made up until late June.

If the beets emerge above ground, cover them with soil to prevent the tops of the roots from becoming dry and tough. Beet leaf-miner larvae can cause unsightly dry, brown blotches from feeding on beet and chard foliage, but healthy plants usually outgrow the damage.

Harvest: For salads, cut chard and beet greens when they are 5 to 10 cm (2 to 4 in.) long. Young chard can be harvested using the cut-and-come-again method.

Harvest mature chard by slicing off the clump above the soil, or pick outer leaves to encourage growth at the centre. A few early greens can be picked from beets, but leave at least two-thirds of the leaves intact if you want to produce sizeable roots.

Probe the soil to determine root size and harvest baby beets at the desired size. Harvest mature beets at the size indicated for the cultivar, usually 5 cm (2 in.) or less in diameter. Lift the roots with a digging fork, and twist off the green tops to prevent desiccation, leaving 2.5 cm (1 in.) stems attached to the root.

Save Seeds: Seed saving is challenging as beets and chard are wind-pollinated and cross-pollinate with each other, in addition to being biennial. Follow the steps in Chapter 3 for collecting seeds of biennials. Chard may survive winter if it is mulched with 15 cm (6 in.) of leaves. When flower stalks emerge, insert a stake near the centre of each plant and enclose the flowers in a cloth bag, supported by the stake. As the fruits dry, strip them by hand from the stalk.

Serve: Slice young beet and chard leaves into ribbons before adding them to salad, and remove chard's thick midrib and chop it separately. Mature greens of both vegetables can be steamed, sautéed, or stir-fried. Beets are essential to *borscht*, a traditional Ukrainian soup. The roots are also delicious roasted, steamed, or boiled until fork-tender.

Preserve: Briefly blanch chard leaves and freeze them like spinach. Preserve beets by canning or pickling them. Cooked beets can be frozen.

Suggested Cultivars

Beets

'Bull's Blood' is an English heirloom with dark crimson leaves that are attractive in *mesclun* mixes and container plantings.

'Chiogga' is an Italian heirloom that reveals candy-striped red and white rings in cross-section. The root doesn't become woody when mature.

'Crosby's Egyptian' is an early-maturing 1885 American heirloom with a large, flat root and long leaves.

'Detroit Dark Red' is a classic American heirloom from 1892.

'Merlin' is a hybrid with good disease resistance and glossy greens.

'Red Ace' is a popular hybrid that is both disease and bolt resistant.

'Rodina' is a 15 cm (6 in.) long, smooth, cylindrical hybrid that yields uniformly sized root slices.

'Touchstone Gold' is a hybrid with reddish skin and a vibrant yellow interior.

Chard

'Bright Lights' is a hybrid that was selected for mild flavour and gorgeous foliage with stems of neon purple, pink, red, yellow, or orange.

'Fordhook Giant' is an heirloom that produces large yields of long, dark green crumpled leaves with white stems.

'Lucullus' is a 1914 heirloom with large, thick, crumpled, light green leaves that are frost resistant and edible into fall.

'Rhubarb' (also known as 'Ruby') is an heirloom, introduced in American gardens in 1857. The plant is relatively short with outstanding red leaf stems and veins.

Carrots

Daucus carota subsp. *sativus*
Family: parsley (*Apiaceae*)
Type: cool-season biennial
Height: 20 cm (8 in.)
Space: 5 to 7.5 cm (2 to 3 in.)
Light: full sun to part shade
Propagation: seed outdoors in early to mid-May
Seed Viability: 3 years

Carrots were domesticated from a flat-topped wildflower species, known as Queen Anne's lace (*Daucus carota*), over two thousand years ago in the area between Afghanistan and Turkey. Early carrots were dark purple with knobby roots; yellow-orange forms evolved later. Orange carrots replaced the purple types on European tables during the Renaissance period. Purple carrots are now marketed as novelty varieties.

Carrots are grouped by shape and root length, and by their use.

'Nelson' carrots

Gardeners favour "Nantes" types because they are sweet and early maturing. Nantes carrots are about 15 cm (6 in.) long and shaped like cylinders with rounded tops and tips. "Chantenay" types are also a home garden favourite: sweet and tender with short, wide-tapered blunt roots. "Danvers" carrots produce thick, broad-shouldered roots and are usually processed into baby food. The typical long, pointed supermarket carrots that store well are known as "Imperator" types. True baby carrots are fast-maturing varieties that produce small roots. Any variety can be harvested small, but the sugars that define flavour develop as carrots mature.

How to Grow: Sow carrots outdoors, two to three weeks before the frost date, in soil that is loose to a depth of at least 30 cm (12 in.). Broadcast the seeds in a patch and rake them into the soil, covering them no more than 0.5 cm (0.25 in.) deep. Apply a thin layer of compost or vermiculite to retain moisture, as carrot seedlings are delicate and have difficulty sprouting through dry soil.

Carrots almost always need to be thinned. Evenly moist soil helps prevent cracked or misshapen roots. Apply compost or hill soil over carrots that rise above the soil line to prevent them from getting "green shoulders," which is caused by exposure to sun-light and makes the top of the root tough and bitter. The overlapping foli-age of carrots that are grown in a patch instead of a row helps shade the soil and prevent greening of the roots.

Carrots can suffer from aster yellows, a virus-like disease that is transmitted by a leafhopper, and the carrot rust fly. Distorted, yellowed foliage and hairy roots are symptoms of aster yellows. Carrot rust flies lay eggs at the base of the young plants and the larvae burrow into the roots, rendering them inedible. A floating row cover installed at planting time is the best preventative measure for both problems. You can also confuse the carrot rust fly, which locates carrot plants by smell, by planting onions nearby.

Harvest: Mature carrots have the best flavour, but the roots can be harvested as soon as they are baby-finger size. Grasp the base of the plant, wiggle it sideways and pull it straight up from the soil, or lift the roots with a digging fork. Twist the leafy tops off, leaving a 2.5 cm (1 in.) stem section attached. Carrots become sweeter after frost, but will spoil if they freeze.

Save Seeds: Follow the measures outlined in Chapter 3 for collecting seeds of biennials, or leave the carrots in the ground and insulate the carrot patch with bales of straw. Since carrots are cross-pollinated by insects, it's necessary to bag the flowers before they open and to hand-pollinate them for pure seed. Remove the bags to pollinate, and replace them until seeds visibly swell. To pollinate, brush a paintbrush across the tops of several flower-heads every morning for two weeks. Collect carrot seeds as they dry and rub them on a screen to remove the tiny hairs.

Serve: Carrots are scrumptious fresh, grated into salads, chopped into stews, steamed, or roasted. A dab of butter and a pinch of fresh, chopped dill perfectly complement steamed carrots.

Preserve: Blanch and freeze carrots or preserve them by canning.

Suggested Cultivars
'Little Finger' is an early-maturing, hybrid baby carrot that can be container-grown.

'Nantes Coreless' is an 1870 heirloom with an orange-red root.

'Nantes Touchon' (also known as 'Touchon') is a French heirloom with bright orange roots.

'Napoli' is a hybrid Nantes type that matures early and withstands cool weather.

'Nelson' is an early-maturing hybrid Nantes type that produces uniform roots.

'Purple Haze' is a hybrid purple carrot with an orange centre. It turns orange throughout when cooked.

'Royal Chantenay' is an open-pollinated, early-maturing orange carrot.

'Scarlet Nantes' (also known as 'Nantes Half Long') is an open-pollinated variety with bright orange roots. Grown in North America for over fifty years, this cultivar established the standard for

comparing garden carrots.
'Thumbelina' is an open-pollinated baby carrot with smooth 2 to 3 cm (1 to 1.5 in.) roots that are round like a ball. It makes a good container plant.

Related Species

Parsnips (*Pastinaca sativa*) are grown for their edible taproots that resemble giant white carrots. The roots are approximately 30 cm (12 in.) long and can be 7.5 cm (3 in.) in diameter at the shoulder. This hardy, biennial plant is cultivated like the carrot except it requires a longer growing season. Use fresh seed each year and sow parsnips outdoors 1 cm (0.5 in.) deep as soon as the ground can be worked in spring. Thin the seedlings 10 cm (4 in.) apart when they are 5 cm (2 in.)

'Andover' parsnips

high. Hard frost improves the sweetness of the roots. Lift them with a digging fork in autumn before the ground freezes, or mulch them and leave them in the ground until late winter (usually March), and harvest them as soon as the ground thaws, just as they start to sprout. Roasting enhances parsnip's sweet flavour.

Suggested Cultivars

'Andover' is a 1984 open-pollinated release from the University of Minnesota. It is disease-resistant and has long, thin roots.

'Gladiator' is a hybrid, disease-resistant, fast-maturing root with smooth skin.

'Harris Model' is an heirloom with large, broad-shouldered roots.

Celeriac and Celery ... For the Enthusiastic Gardener

Apium graveolens var. *rapaceum* and *Apium graveolens* var. *dulce*

Family: parsley (*Apiaceae*)
Type: Cool-season biennial
Height: 30 to 45 cm (12 to 18 in.)
Space: 20 cm (8 in.)
Light: full sun to part shade
Propagation: seed indoors in late February, transplant outdoors after the frost date
Seed Viability: retains 50% germination for 5 years

Celeriac and celery are different varieties of the same plant; celeriac is grown for its enlarged, knobby stem at and beneath the soil, while celery was selected for long, succulent leaf stems. Celery was domesticated first, from a wild marsh plant native to Europe and Asia. It's challenging to cultivate because plenty of water and cool weather are necessary to produce tender, mild stems. Celeriac has a similar flavour and is much easier to grow as it tolerates a wider range of conditions. Both crops require a long season to produce.

How to Grow: Celeriac and celery must be set outdoors as transplants. Sow both indoors ten weeks before the frost date. Before sowing the seeds, soak them for six hours, rinse them and discard the water. Light promotes germination, so cover the seeds lightly and keep them moist, using a clear plastic cover to raise humidity. Germination can take up to three weeks.

Harden off celeriac or celery seedlings by restricting irrigation instead of exposing them to cold temperatures, because chilly temperatures can cause them to bolt prematurely. For this reason, it's best to plant them outdoors after the frost date, usually in late May. Both plants tolerate afternoon shade, and celery needs consistently moist soil throughout the growing season. Celeriac can be grown in a pot, but containers dry out too quickly to produce quality celery. The growth form of both plants complements lettuce.

Harvest: Harvest celeriac when the base of the plant reaches 5 cm (2 in.)

'Large Smooth Prague' celeriac

Celery plants require consistently moist soil to produce tender stems.

in diameter, before a hard frost. Lift it from the soil with a garden fork, and cut the leafy tops from the base.

Harvest celery when the stems reach the desired size by cutting the plant off just above the soil line, keeping the stems connected at the base. Refrigerate the stalks upright in a jar with 2.5 cm (1 in.) of water, changing the water daily.

Save Seeds: It's challenging to over-winter celery indoors without drying the roots. Success is more likely with celeriac, using the method for saving seeds of biennials in Chapter 3. The plant sends up a flat flowerhead of tiny blossoms; collect the seeds as they dry by shaking the head into a paper bag.

Serve: The green leaves and stalks of celery and celeriac can be chopped and used in soups, stews, or salads, although celeriac greens are better cooked since they are tougher and stronger tasting. Prepare the knobby base of celeriac by peeling it to reveal the creamy white interior, and prevent browning of the cut surfaces by placing it in a bowl of water with a few tablespoons of lemon juice or white vinegar. It can be eaten raw, grated in salads, or chopped into thin sticks and served on a vegetable platter. It is also good cooked and mashed with potatoes, roasted, or added to soups, stews, and stir-fries.

Suggested Cultivars
Celeriac
'Large Smooth Prague' is a widely available, popular open-pollinated variety.
Celery
'Tall Utah 52-70' is open-pollinated, compact and bolt-resistant.
'Ventura' is open-pollinated and productive, and has some heat tolerance.

Chervil
Anthriscus cerefolium
Family: parsley (*Apiaceae*)
Type: cool-season annual
Height: 30 to 45 cm (12 to18 in.)
Space: 15 to 22.5 cm (6 to 9 in.)
Light: part shade preferred, full sun to shade

Chervil seedlings

Propagation: seed outdoors in early spring

Seed Viability: retains 50% germination for 3 years

A native of southeastern Europe and western Asia, chervil features finely cut, ferny foliage and flat flowerheads of tiny white blossoms. It exudes a faint aroma of licorice, but its dainty leaves are highly perishable when fresh, and their anise flavour is lost when dried, so it's essential to grow this plant if you like its exquisite flavour.

How to Grow: Chervil grows from a taproot that does not transplant well. It is sown directly outdoors in early spring, as soon as the soil can be worked. Press the seeds into the soil, but do not cover them completely as light promotes germination. Germination takes two to three weeks and the plant grows best when daytime temperatures hover near 13°C (55°F). It quickly runs to seed with heat. Chervil makes a great container plant.

Harvest: Pluck or clip leaves from the outside of the plant just before use.

Save Seeds: Collect the narrow, pointed seeds as they become dark brown and dry, atop the flat heads. Chervil readily self-seeds in the garden.

Serve: Chervil is cherished in French cuisine as part of the fresh *fines herbes* mixture (with parsley, chives, and tarragon) and it adds a pleasant hint of licorice when tossed with greens such as baby lettuces and arugula. Chervil makes a lovely herbal butter.

Preserve: The best way to extend chervil's culinary life is chopped and blended into butter or frozen as a *fines herbs* mixture.

Chicory and Endive

Cichorium intybus and *Cichorium endivia*

Family: sunflower (*Asteraceae*)

Type: cool-season biennial

Height: up to 30 cm (12 in.)

Space: 7.5 cm (3 in.) for baby greens, 15 to 22 cm (6 to 9 in.) for mature greens

'Chioggia' type chicory

Leaf or "cutting" chicory is harvested using the cut-and-come-again method.

'Full Heart Batavian' endive

Light: full sun to part shade
Propagation: seed chicory outdoors in early May; seed endive outdoors in early May or in late June; both species can be sown indoors in early April and transplanted outdoors in mid-May
Seed Viability: 8 years

Chicory and endive originate from the Mediterranean region, where they have been cultivated since Egyptian times. They are closely related and both produce bitter greens that are very popular in Europe. These gourmet greens are usually mixed with other salad ingredients to balance their tangy flavour.

Chicory is especially versatile; there are several different types, and many cultivated varieties. The kind known as radicchio produces small heads that can be round like a miniature cabbage (called "Chioggia" types) or upright like a tiny Romaine lettuce (called "Trevisio" types). Chicories that form open, leafy rosettes or long dandelion-shaped greens are referred to as "cutting chicories" as the young greens are harvested using the cut-and-come-again method. Other types are grown for their roots, which are dried and brewed into a beverage, grated fresh

into salads, or cultivated in a specialized manner to produce a gourmet salad green known as Belgian endive.

Endive varieties are of two types: curly leaved, and a larger broad-leaved form known as 'Batavian' endive or escarole. Both form a head of dark green outer leaves and pale green inner leaves: those with broader leaves are hardier, while the types with frilly foliage are more heat tolerant. Endive becomes sweeter with cool weather, so it is often grown as a late-season crop.

How to Grow: Seed directly outdoors, 0.5 cm (0.25 in.) deep or rake seeds into the soil, two weeks before the frost date. Or seed indoors, six weeks before the frost date and transplant seedlings outdoors near the frost date. Press the seeds into the planting mix and barely cover them, as light promotes germination. For fall crops, sow the seeds directly outdoors in late June.

Chicory and endive may bolt prematurely if the weather is hot as the days become long, or if young plants are exposed to night temperatures below 5°C (41°F). Mature plants are resistant to frost, pests and diseases, but are intolerant of summer heat unless they receive plenty of moisture or afternoon shade.

Endive is blanched in the garden one week before the head is harvested, by tying the outer leaves loosely together over the head or by placing an upturned clay pot or cardboard box over the plant. Blanching bleaches the inner leaves to a pale, creamy yellow and produces milder flavour. To prevent rot, be sure the leaves are dry before blanching them.

Harvest: Harvest salad greens when chicory and endive leaves are 5 to 10 cm (2 to 4 in.) long, by plucking them or by the cut-and-come-again method. Harvest mature chicory and endive heads when they reach the size indicated for the variety, by cutting the rosette of leaves off the stalk, and discard the tough, bitter outer leaves. Both are frost tolerant, and can be protected for late fall harvests.

Save Seeds: To save endive seeds, lift the plants in autumn and follow the instructions in chapter 3 for saving seeds of biennials. Allow seed pods to dry on the plant the following year. Endive is self-pollinating and its seed will not be affected if chicory is grown nearby, but it will cross-pollinate with chicory and ruin the chicory seed.

Some chicory cultivars will survive prairie winters if mulched. The second year, chicory produces sky-blue or white flowers, which look like those of the roadside weed that is the same species. (The wild species is also edible, but cultivated varieties have better flavour). Endive flowers look similar. Allow the seed-heads to mature on the plant and collect small, fluffy seeds when they change colour and start to dry. Hardy chicory cultivars self sow in the garden.

Serve: Endive is mainly used in salad mixes. It can also be served as a steamed vegetable or included in soups. Chicory leaves are used in salads and soups, stir-fried with other vegetables or fried in olive oil with garlic and lemon. When using chicory leaves, the thick mid rib is removed and chopped separately to contribute a crunchy texture.

Preserve: Chicory leaves can be frozen after blanching them briefly in a pot of boiling water with a spoonful of salt.

Suggested Cultivars
Chicory
'Chioggia' is an Italian heirloom radicchio variety with burgundy-tinged foliage.
'Catalogna' is open-pollinated and resembles a giant dandelion with long, serrated leaves.
'Grumolo' is open-pollinated and forms frost-hardy rosettes of smooth, rounded leaves for cutting.
'Indigo' is an early-maturing, hybrid radicchio type that produces maroon foliage with white veins.
'Sugarloaf' is an open-pollinated

variety that forms a tall, upright clump.

Endive

'Full Heart Batavian' is a popular open-pollinated variety with broad leaves and mild flavour.

'Green Curled Ruffec' is open-pollinated and has very frilly leaves.

For the Enthusiastic Gardener ...

Belgian Endive or *witlof* (Dutch for "white leaves") is a chicory type that is cultivated in two stages. It is sown outdoors to develop a root, and then the root is forced indoors to produce a compact, bleached leafy bud called a "chicon." Sow Belgian endive outdoors in mid-May, and thin the seedlings to 10 cm (4 in.) apart. In autumn, lift the carrot-like roots before the soil freezes, usually in late October. Trim the roots to 20 cm (8 in.) and cut off the leaves, leaving a 4 cm (2 in.) stem attached. The roots can be stored for several months, refrigerated in a perforated plastic bag. To force them to produce desirable buds, plant about twelve roots upright in a bucket or pot with drainage holes, with 15 cm (6 in.) of moist soil or sand beneath them. Cover the bucket with a damp towel or black plastic garbage bag (open every few days for air exchange) and store it in complete darkness, with a temperature range of 12°C to 18°C (55°F to 65°F). It takes about three to four weeks to produce. Harvest the pale buds when they are 10 cm (4 in.) long. They should be refrigerated and used within a few days. Serve with the core partially removed as an individual gourmet salad, with dark greens and a vinaigrette dressing, or quarter the buds and bake them topped with cheese and breadcrumbs.

Suggested Cultivar

'Bruxelles Witloof' is a European heirloom.

Cilantro, Coriander

Coriandrum sativum

Family: parsley (*Apiaceae*)
Type: cool-season annual
Height: 30 to 45 cm (12 to 18 in.)
Space: 20 cm (8 in.)
Light: partial shade to full sun
Propagation: seed outdoors in early to mid-May
Seed Viability: 2 years

Cilantro

This plant bears two separate names; cilantro refers to the leaves and the seeds are known as coriander. Native to southern Europe and the eastern Mediterranean region, it has been cultivated for over a thousand years. Its seeds are used to spice sausages, pickles, and curries, while the sharp taste of the greens adds zest to Asian and Mexican dishes. Some people find the unique leaf flavour unpleasantly "soapy."

How to Grow: Direct seed cilantro outdoors 0.5 cm (0.25 in.) deep, and cover the seeds completely as darkness is required for germination. The plant arises from a taproot and it may bolt if transplanted. Cilantro is short-lived and blossoms in response to warm weather and long days. As the flat, white blossom clusters are pollinated, they develop small, round fruits containing the seed crop. If you are growing it primarily for foliage, sow seeds in succession every three weeks until mid-July to extend the harvest, and to have a supply when other salsa ingredients such as tomatoes, peppers, and onions are ripe at the end of the season. Cilantro can be grown in containers.

Harvest: Pluck the larger lower leaves when the plants are 15 cm (6 in.). Cilantro produces finely dissected, bitter upper leaves as it matures. To harvest coriander seeds, allow the fruits to ripen on the plant so that they develop a spicy aroma, and pick them as soon as they turn light brown and dry. The seeds shatter easily once mature.

Save Seeds: Collect ripe seeds or allow cilantro to self-seed in the garden.

Serve: Cilantro is quite perishable and heat diminishes its flavour; it's best to use leaves fresh or add them at the end of cooking. Cilantro is an ingredient of classic Mexican salsa. Fresh flowers can also be tossed in a salad. Coriander seeds are used whole or crushed. The pungent aroma of the seeds can be enhanced by briefly toasting them in a dry pan before crushing them.

Preserve: Store dry coriander seeds in a cool, dark cupboard.

Suggested Cultivars
'Delfino' is open-pollinated and has unique, finely dissected foliage.
'Santo' is open-pollinated and bolt-resistant; it produces large leaves.

Dill
Anethum graveolens
Family: parsley (*Apiaceae*)
Type: cool-season annual
Height: 45 to 90 cm (18 to 36 in.) or taller
Space: 15 cm (6 in.) for greens; 30 cm (12 in.) for seeds
Light: full sun to part shade
Propagation: seed outdoors in early to mid-May
Seed Viability: retains 50% germination for 5 years

Dill

Dill is a tall, ferny plant with flat blossom heads, characteristic of the parsley family. The foliage, flowers, and seeds of this versatile herb have culinary use. Although it originated in Europe, dill has naturalized in many parts of the world after being cultivated for thousands of years.

How to Grow: Sow dill seed directly outdoors in early to mid-May. Light stimulates germination; press the seeds into the soil and barely cover them. Germination usually takes a couple weeks. Small dill seedlings can be transplanted if the taproot is handled carefully. The plant flowers in response to heat, long days, and when it reaches maturity. If your aim is to produce mainly greens, extend the harvest by sowing seeds in succession every three weeks during spring.

Harvest: Clip or pick leaves at the desired size, just before use. Flower heads are usually harvested when half the flowers open. As seeds develop, they can be collected for kitchen use or to plant in the garden.

Save Seeds: Dill seeds shatter easily from the plant when ripe and will self-seed in the garden. To collect them, enclose the entire seed-head in a paper or cloth bag as the seeds swell and turn brown. When dry, clip the head or shake the seeds into the bag.

Serve: Dill is excellent for flavouring pickles, potatoes, and seafood. Use fresh leaves in soups, salad dressings, and sauces, but add them after cooking as heat destroys their essence. Entire flower heads or seed heads are useful in pickling recipes and dried seeds add a piquant flavour to vegetable dishes and potato salad.

Preserve: Dill leaves become bland when dried; freezing retains better flavour. Simply freeze the leafy stems in an airtight container, and snap off frozen bits when needed and add them directly to your recipe. Store dry seeds in a cool, dark cupboard.

Suggested Cultivars
'Bouquet' is an early, open-pollinated variety grown for its large seed-heads.

'Fernleaf' is bolt-resistant, open-pollinated, and desirable for leaf production. At 45 cm (18 in.), its dwarf form is ideal for containers.

Related Species

Sweet Fennel (*Foeniculum vulgare* v. *dulce)* and Florence Fennel (*Foeniculum vulgare* v. *azoricum*) are tender cool-season perennial herbs that are treated as annuals and grown like dill. Both have ferny foliage that is anise-scented. Florence fennel is also known as *finocchio*. It produces edible leaves and a succulent swollen bulb at the base of its leaf stalks.

Sweet fennel and Florence fennel are sown 0.5 cm (0.25 in.) deep, outdoors in early to mid-May. Thin the seedlings to 30 cm (12 in.) apart, and remove any seed stalks that form. Either type of fennel can be grown in containers. Harvest sweet fennel by clipping foliage at the desired size just before using it. Lift Florence fennel with a digging fork when the base thickens to about 5 cm (2 in.) in diameter, and trim off the leaves and roots. Both types of fennel can be started earlier indoors and transplanted in late May if the roots are handled carefully. Disturbing the taproot may cause the plants to bolt. Fresh sweet fennel foliage is used in herbal vinegar, to flavour fish, and as a salad ingredient or garnish. Florence fennel tastes delicious roasted, boiled, or sliced raw on a vegetable platter or salad.

Sweet fennel

Florence fennel

The curly scape of hardneck garlic is considered a delicacy.

Probe the soil to check garlic bulb formation.

Suggested Cultivars

'Bronze Fennel Smokey' sweet fennel is open-pollinated, bolt-resistant and has beautiful copper foliage.

'Zefa Fino' is a bolt-resistant, open-pollinated Florence fennel that produces large bulbs.

'Orion' is a bolt-resistant hybrid Florence fennel that produces large bulbs.

Garlic

Allium sativum

Family: onion (*Alliaceae*)
Type: cool-season bulb
Height: 90 cm (36 in.)
Space: 15 cm (6 in.)
Light: full sun to partial shade
Propagation: plant cloves outdoors in September

Garlic has been cultivated for thousands of years. Wild garlic came from mountainous regions of central Asia, where summers are hot and dry, and winters long and severe. The plant grows from an underground bulb made up of specialized leaves. The leaves swell to form thick cloves that are tightly wrapped together in a papery sheath.

Garlic cultivars are generally grouped according to whether they possess a woody flowering stalk, called a scape. True flowers are rarely produced on the stiff stalk; a capsule of miniature aerial cloves known as bulbils develops instead. Types that produce a scape are known as "hardneck" garlic, while those that don't are referred to as "softneck." Hardneck garlic bulbs are composed of a few very large cloves that are more intensely flavoured than softneck types, and the plants are sturdier and hardier. Softneck cultivars are more typical of supermarket fare. Softneck bulbs contain many small cloves and pliable foliage that is easily braided into decorative strands; the stiff neck of hardneck garlic is difficult to bend and challenging to braid.

How to Grow: Plant garlic in autumn, at least six weeks before the ground freezes, usually during September. To initiate bulb formation, the plants need six to eight weeks of temperatures below 4°C (40°F). By the time the ground can be worked in spring, there isn't enough cold weather to trigger the bulbing process; cloves that are planted in spring will yield greens, but not large bulbs. Fall-planted cloves emerge very early in spring, and bulbs begin to form when the day-length reaches thirteen hours and soil temperatures are above 16°C (60°F).

Separate garlic cloves and plant them with the point facing up and covered with 5 cm (2 in.) of soil. Locally grown bulbs can be used for planting stock, but planting grocery store garlic is a gamble. In regions with extreme winter temperatures or inconsistent snow cover, apply straw mulch 8 to 10 cm (3 to 4 in.) deep to insulate the cloves. The mulch can either be removed in mid-April or left to retain moisture and control weeds.

Mulch slows soil warming in spring, which slightly delays the crop.

Research has shown that hardneck types produce larger bulbs when the curly scape is removed about ten days after it appears. However, there is also evidence that the bulbs keep longer with the scape intact until harvest.

To ready garlic for harvest, stop irrigating it as soon as the plants begin to turn yellow.

Harvest: Lift garlic bulbs with a digging fork when half the plant's foliage becomes yellow and dry. Cure the bulbs on newspaper in a dark, well-ventilated place for at least two weeks, until the skins dry. After drying, clean them by peeling off the outermost layers. The cloves bruise easily if separated, so keep each bulb intact and protected with its papery sheath. Trim the roots and remove the woody stem 2.5 cm (1 in.) above the bulb. Store cured garlic bulbs in a mesh bag or

Cured hardneck garlic bulbs

open container in a dark cupboard at room temperature.

Save Seeds: Bulbs from your summer crop can be planted the same fall for next year's crop. Large cloves produce the largest bulbs. If planted, the tiny bulbils atop the scape produce edible greens the following spring; each bulbil can form a full-size bulb in two to three years.

Serve: Garlic's unique zest is released when the cloves are cut. Press the clove with the flat side of a knife until the skin cracks to make it easier to peel before chopping. Heat reduces garlic's bite and roasting mellows its sharpness enough to serve it as a spread on toasted bread. To roast, slice the tops off unpeeled bulbs and drizzle the cut surface with olive oil, then place them in a 400°F oven for about 30 minutes until soft. Allow bulbs to cool and pry the creamy cloves out of their skins with a small knife. Garlic scapes are considered a delicacy steamed and served with melted butter, or chopped and included in a stir-fry.

Suggested Cultivars

'German Extra-Hardy' is a hardneck type with large cloves and dark reddish brown skin.

'Hutterite' is a hardy, softneck type with small cloves and creamy white skin.

'Music' is a hardneck type that produces high yields of large bulbs.

'Spanish Roja' is a hardneck type with large cloves and purple-streaked skin.

Kale ... and Related Cole Crops

Brassica oleracea var. *acephala*
Family: mustard (*Brassicaceae*)
Type: cool-season biennial
Height: 30 to 45 cm (12 to 18 in.)
Space: 30 cm (12 in.)
Light: full sun
Propagation: seed outdoors in early to mid-May; seed indoors in early April and transplant outdoors in mid May
Seed Viability: 4 years

Kale sprang from a Mediterranean wild cabbage that eventually evolved into an assortment of vegetables,

'Red Russian' kale

including broccoli, Brussels sprouts, head cabbage, cauliflower, and kohlrabi. This group demonstrates how one plant can be remarkably changed by selection to emphasize different plant parts. In England, kale was known as "cole" and these cabbage cousins are collectively referred to as "cole crops." Chinese cabbages (*Brassica rapa*) are related to this group, but their origins were in Asia; some cultivars are described in this chapter as *mesclun* greens.

Of the cole crops, kale is easiest to grow. Cabbage and kohlrabi are also widely grown, but the others are more challenging; cauliflower is fussy; Brussels sprouts need a long season to produce; and broccoli is easily grown, but it can be a magnet for bugs.

Cole crops attract insect pests that render their various edible parts unappetizing. Nearby fields of related canola and mustard supply a reservoir of insects that move into home gardens. Shiny flea beetles attack seedlings in spring, leave "shot-holes" in the leaves and produce offspring that eat plant roots; green cabbageworms chew large holes in leaves; and white root maggots girdle seedling stems and chomp on roots later in the season. To make matters worse, some larvae leave excrement on the crop and their feeding damage opens the plants to disease. The best organic control measures are to use floating row covers, and to grow these crops from transplants.

How to Grow: Seed kale outdoors as the soil temperature reaches 13°C (55°F), or sow seeds in individual pots four weeks before the frost date and transplant them outdoors near the frost date. Kale is an ornamental plant and quite suitable for container culture.

In areas where insect pests attack emerging seedlings, it's better to set out four-week-old transplants, which are stronger and can outgrow the damage. Cover your seedlings with floating row covers at planting time to provide a barrier against flea beetles and to restrict other insects from laying eggs near your plants.

Harvest: Pick individual leaves as needed, at the size you prefer, from the outside of the plant.

Save Seeds: Follow the instructions for saving seeds of biennials in Chapter 3, and harvest the pods as they dry. Saving pure seeds from kale and other biennial cole crops is challenging, as many cross-pollinate with each other.

Serve: Enjoy kale's earthy flavour roasted, in soups, or in stir-fries. Young leaves add crunchy texture to a salad, and flower buds and young seedpods are also edible.

Preserve: Blanch kale leaves and freeze them.

Suggested Cultivars

'Winterbor' is a frost hardy, tall, dark blue-green hybrid.

'Red Russian' is an heirloom with wavy, grey-green leaves and purplish leaf veins.

Related Species

Cabbage (*Brassica oleracea* var. *capitata*) is seeded 1 cm (0.5 in.) deep, outdoors in early to mid-May or set outdoors as a four-week-old transplant in early to late May. The plants can take some frost. Space transplants 30 to 45 cm (12 to 18 in.) apart, depending on the cultivar. When the cabbage reaches the size indicated for the variety, pull back the outer leaves and cut it off, just below its base. Cabbage leaves can be used to make cabbage rolls, or served boiled, or sliced in salads and stir-fries. Some cabbage cultivars are appropriate for long-term storage, but cabbage does not freeze well.

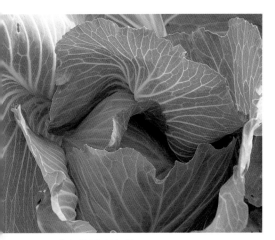

'Late Flat Dutch' cabbage

Suggested Cultivars

'Dynamo' is an early-maturing hybrid that produces a small, blue-green head.

'Late Flat Dutch' is a late-maturing, open-pollinated cultivar that produces an enormous, flat green head that stores well.

'Minicole' is a mid-season hybrid that produces uniform green heads.

'Savoy Express' is an early-maturing hybrid that produces a yellowish-green crinkly-leaved head.

'Super Red 80' is an early-maturing hybrid with a deep purplish-red head.

Kohlrabi (*Brassica oleracea* var. *gongylodes*) is a biennial that is seeded outdoors 1 cm (0.5 in.) deep, in early to mid-May. The seedlings should be thinned 10 cm (4 in.) apart. Kohlrabi can be grown in containers. Harvest by digging when the swollen stems reach 2.5 cm to 7.5 cm (1 to 3 in.) in diameter, and trim the leaves and roots off. Serve kohlrabi sliced in salads, roasted, or boiled and mashed similar to turnips. Kohlrabi slices or cubes can be blanched and frozen or preserved as pickles.

Suggested Cultivars

'Early White Vienna' is open-pollinated and pale green.

'Kolibri' is a hybrid with a brilliant purple stem.

'Kolibri' kohlrabi

Brussels sprouts form along a tall stem, topped by a clump of leaves.

Broccoli

Related Species ... For the Enthusiastic Gardener

Broccoli (*Brassica oleracea* var. *italica*) is seeded outdoors in early to mid-May or set out as four-week-old seedlings, spaced 30 cm (12 in.) apart, in early to late May. Harvest by cutting the central head of flower buds while it is firm. Side shoots with smaller heads can be harvested for a second crop. Homegrown broccoli is delicious when steamed lightly or served on a fresh vegetable platter. Broccoli can be blanched and frozen.

Suggested Cultivars

'Green Comet' is an early-maturing and heat-tolerant hybrid.
'Arcadia' is a mid-season hybrid that produces large, firm heads.

Brussels Sprouts (*Brassica oleracea* var. *gemmifera*) need a long season to form edible sprouts along the stem. Set four- to six-week-old transplants outdoors in mid to late May and space them 60 cm (24 in.) apart. The sprouts mature from the base upward and are harvested when they are firm and about 2.5 cm (1 in.) in size. Steam Brussels sprouts and toss them with butter and Parmesan cheese, or roast them until tender. Brussels sprouts can be blanched and frozen.

Suggested Cultivar

'Oliver' is an early-maturing hybrid.

Cauliflower (*Brassica oleracea* var. *botrytis*) should be set outdoors as a four- to six-week-old transplant, spaced 45 cm (18in.) apart in mid to late May. It's often blanched in the garden by tying the outer leaves over the head as it forms. Harvest the head

Leeks

Cauliflower is challenging to grow.

when it is firm and reaches the size indicated for the variety. Serve cauliflower florets steamed or on a fresh vegetable platter. Cauliflower can be blanched and frozen.

Suggested Cultivar

'Minuteman' is an early-maturing hybrid with a white head.

Leeks

Allium ampeloprasum var. *porrum*
Family: onion (*Alliaceae*)
Type: cool-season biennial
Height: 45 cm (18 in.)
Space: 10 to 15 cm (4 to 6 in.)
Light: full sun to partial shade
Propagation: seed indoors in late February, transplant seedlings outdoors near frost date
Seed Viability: retains 50% germination for 3 years

Leeks probably originated from a Mediterranean wild onion. The plant forms a succulent cylinder of bundled leaf sheaths that unfolds in a fan of flat, blue-green leaves. It was cultivated and prized for its mild flavour by ancient Egyptian, Greek, and Roman cultures. According to legend, the plant became a symbol of Wales after a victorious 7th century battle, where leeks adorned the helmets of Welsh soldiers to distinguish them from their Saxon foes.

How to grow: Leeks require a long growing season and should be sown indoors in late February. Transplant the seedlings outdoors just before the frost date.

Traditionally, leeks are blanched in the garden to increase their edible white portion. This is usually done by planting them in a shallow trench and hilling them with 5 to 8 cm (2 to 4 in.) of soil as they grow. Seedlings can be planted close together if their leaf fans are placed parallel. The new leaves emerge opposite each other and directly above the previous ones. Leeks look beautiful planted next to chard or lettuce; their tall, sleek stems complement rosettes of crinkly leaves.

Harvest: Harvest leeks before the first fall frost, at the size you prefer, from the pencil-thin baby leek stage until they form fat 5 cm (2 in.) stalks. Gently lift them from the soil with a digging fork and brush the soil off the roots. Refrigerate leeks unwashed and untrimmed.

Save Seeds: If mulched, hardy leek cultivars survive winter to bloom the second year after planting. The plant sends up a tall flowering stalk, topped by an ornamental globe of small radiating florets, which are pollinated by bees. Pick the round pods when they are brown and dry. Shake or rub them to extract the dark seeds.

Serve: The base of the leek is the edible portion, used to make a classic soup. Prepare it by trimming off the roots and all but 5 cm (2 in.) of the green tops, and cutting the tender white base in half. Rinse each half thoroughly, separating the layers to remove soil particles that became trapped between them as the plant grew. Young leeks are used like scallions. The tough, green leaves and young, green seedpods are useful to flavour soup stock. Leeks should be used fresh; they become mushy and bitter when frozen.

Suggested Cultivars

'Large American Flag' (also known as 'Broad London') is an heirloom with long, thick stalks.
'Giant Musselbergh' is a hardy, late-maturing heirloom with large stalks.

Lettuce

Lactuca sativa
Family: sunflower (*Asteraceae*)
Type: cool-season annual
Height: up to 30 cm (12 in.)
Space: 7.5 cm (3 in.) for baby greens, 15 to 22 cm (6 to 9 in.) for mature heads
Light: full sun to part shade

SIMPLE LEEK SOUP

Combine equal portions of chopped leeks and potatoes with enough water to cover them. Simmer until tender, and puree the mixture, adding water if necessary to obtain the desired soup consistency. Season with salt and pepper.

'Paris Island Cos' lettuce

'Red Sails' lettuce

Propagation: seed indoors in early April and transplant outdoors in mid-May or seed outdoors in early May
Seed Viability: 5 years

Lettuce likely came from a wild prickly species (*Lactuca serriola*), which was used as a medicinal herb by ancient Mediterranean cultures. It was domesticated so long ago that no similar plant is known today in the wild. The Greeks and Romans cultivated lettuce as a salad green, and it's pictured on the walls of Egyptian tombs dating back to 4500 BCE. Its name is derived from *lactis*, Latin for "milk," referring to the plant's white sap.

The best lettuce types for prairie gardens include butterhead, cos, or Romaine and leaf lettuce. Butterheads, also known as Bibb or Boston lettuce, form rosettes of creamy, succulent leaves. Cos lettuce produces an upright cluster of sturdy, crisp leaves; it was dubbed "Romaine" after being introduced to France from Rome, although it originated on the Greek island of Cos. Leaf lettuce forms loose, fluffy clumps of tender leaves. Due to their perishable nature and ease of cultivation, leaf lettuces are most popular among gardeners.

Lettuce rosettes are very attractive plants for the front of edible borders. An infinite choice of cultivars comes in all hues of green and red, including speckled mixtures of both, and the leaf shapes can be frilly, lobed, pointed, or scalloped.

How to Grow: Seed lettuce 0.5 cm (0.25 in.) deep or rake the seeds into the soil when the soil temperature reaches 4°C (40°F). Light promotes germination of some lettuces. Choose bolt-resistant cultivars for early sowings. To extend the harvest, sow a new crop of lettuce when the seedlings from the previous sowing have sprouted.

Lettuce can be seeded indoors four to six weeks ahead of transplanting outdoors, and it can be grown outdoors as a container plant.

Lettuce germinates rapidly at room temperature, but seeds may become dormant if the temperature exceeds 27°F (80°F). To boost outdoor germination during hot weather, pre-treat your seeds between damp paper towels or moist vermiculite in a plastic bag in the refrigerator for five days before planting them outdoors. This cool, moist treatment will initiate germination, causing the seed to swell slightly, and it can be sown directly outdoors.

Alternately, set transplants outdoors and buffer the plants from heat with afternoon shade and moist soil.

Keep the soil evenly moist, particularly if your aim is to produce baby greens, and apply compost mulch around the plants between "cut-and-come-again" crops.

Lettuce that is sown early enough to develop with lengthening days may be triggered to bloom before it reaches its potential size. Later sowings that mature with shorter days can produce bigger heads before bolting.

Harvest: Cut lettuce from its stem at the desired leaf size. For baby greens, pick leaves from the outer edges of the plant or snip them using the "cut-and-come-again" method.

Save Seeds: Allow the plant to bolt and send up a tall seed stalk. Lettuce is both self-pollinated and pollinated by insects, but the flowers on each head open for only one day. When ripe, the seeds look like tiny dandelion seeds and can be shaken from the stalk into a paper bag. Rub them between your fingers to remove the fluff and dry them overnight on a screen.

Serve: Blend baby lettuce with other spicy greens, herbs, and edible flowers for an elaborate mixture, or enjoy a crisp lettuce salad with a simple vinaigrette dressing.

Suggested Cultivars
Butterhead
'Buttercrunch' forms a large, loose head with thick, medium green leaves. It's open-pollinated, slow to bolt, disease-resistant, and tolerant of heat and cold. It can be sown in late October for a spring crop.

'Esmeralda' is bright green, open-pollinated, slow to bolt, and disease-resistant.

'Tom Thumb' is an English heirloom from the 1830s with green outer leaves and a creamy yellow interior. Its baseball-size head makes it the perfect size for containers.

Cos (Romaine):
'Freckles' is open-pollinated and bolt-resistant. Its green foliage has burgundy splotches.

'Little Gem' forms a bright green head, small enough for an individual

SIMPLE VINAIGRETTE
• •

A simple dressing is the perfect accent to highlight your fresh garden greens.

One part acid (vinegar, herbal vinegar, or lemon juice);
Three parts oil (olive or canola)

Combine both ingredients in a lidded jar and shake vigorously. Serve.

salad. It is open-pollinated and makes an ideal container plant.

'Paris Island Cos' is a French heirloom from 1868 that forms a robust head with deep green leaves.

'Rouge d'Hiver' is a French heirloom from the 1840s. Its leaves are copper-red with green at the base. The plant tolerates heat and cold, and can be grown into autumn if it's protected from frost with a row cover.

Leaf

'Black Seeded Simpson' is a fast-maturing, heat-tolerant heirloom from 1850 with light green leaves.

'Deer Tongue' is a 1740s heirloom with triangular green leaves. It tolerates heat and cold, and can be grown into autumn if it's protected from frost with a row cover.

'Lollo Rossa' is open-pollinated, heat-resistant, compact, and deeply frilled with a green interior and rosy red leaf edges.

'Merlot' is open-pollinated and produces deep purplish red frilly leaves.

'Oak Leaf' is an heirloom cultivar, dating before 1900. It is heat-tolerant and forms ornamental, loose clumps of lime green lobed leaves.

'Red Sails' forms a broad, open head with frilly maroon leaves. It is open-pollinated, slow to bolt, and heat-tolerant.

'Salad Bowl' is open-pollinated, bolt-resistant and produces frilly, deeply lobed, lime green leaves.

Mesclun Greens

Mesclun is derived from the Latin for "mixture" and combines a variety of young salad leaves from different plants. It originates from the European practice of gathering greens in the wild. Contemporary *mesclun* mixes intermingle tangy European and Asian greens with a base of mild-tasting, decorative lettuces. Straight from the garden, a medley of mesclun greens can create a sensory experience that raises the simple salad to a fine art.

Mesclun greens are valued as the first fresh pickings of the season. Most are cool-season plants that become intensely spicy and unpalatable as summer approaches. Mesclun species are often marketed as a seed mix, but it's

Mesclun greens

better to cultivate each type separately to distinguish them from weeds, and to identify which ones that you find most appealing. In addition, some types grow faster and will outcompete others.

How to Grow: Sow a few seeds of each species; mesclun greens grow fast and are used in small amounts. The seeds of most species will remain viable for future sowings within four years. Choose a location with full sun to partial shade and seed directly outdoors 0.5 cm (0.25 in.) deep in early spring as soon as the soil can be worked, or sow in late October for an early crop the following spring. Mesclun greens can be cultivated in containers, too.

Thin the plants to 7.5 to 10 cm (3 to 4 in.) apart when the seedlings are 5 cm (2-in.) tall and maintain an evenly moist soil. As the weather warms and the plants mature, the flavour of many becomes bitter, hot, and unpalatable. Remove and compost spent plants and plant a warm-season crop such as bush beans in their place.

Harvest: Harvest mesclun greens when the leaves are 5 to 10 cm (2 to 4 in.) long by picking outer leaves from the plant, or use the cut-and-come-again method. If the weather remains cool, new leaves that sprout from the stem will be palatable enough for a second picking.

Serve: Combine one or two attractive lettuces with two or three mesclun greens. Chicory, endive, beet greens,

Arugula leaves add a peppery flavour to salads.

Mizuna

Garden cress

Corn salad

Pak choi

chard, and spinach, as well as a sprinkling of fresh herbs, such as chervil, sorrel, or parsley also make excellent salad partners. Edible flower petals can be added for colour. Dress your salad creation with a simple vinaigrette.

Suggested Mesclun Species (most cultivars are open-pollinated):
mustard family (*Brassicaceae*)
Arugula (*Eruca vesicaria* ssp. *sativa*) has dark green, deeply lobed leaves and a piquant flavour. Its white flowers and peppery seed-pods are also used to spice up salads.
Garden Cress (*Lepidium sativum*) is available in several varieties with dainty rounded or curly leaves.
Mizuna (*Brassica rapa* ssp. *nipposinica*)

is a Japanese heirloom with mild flavour and a decorative, finely cut leaf.
Mustard (*Brassica juncea*) tastes peppery. 'Osaka Purple' is a Japanese heirloom cultivar with violet-green leaves.
Pak Choi (*Brassica rapa* var. *chinensis*) is a type of Chinese cabbage that forms an upright cluster of spoon-shaped leaves rather than a tight head.

purslane family (*Portulacaceae*)
Miner's Lettuce (*Montia perfoliata*) is a tiny frost-tolerant plant made up of a pair of fused leaves that encircle a stem topped by delicate white flowers. It tastes similar to spinach. It grows wild in forests of western North America, and prefers partial shade.

sunflower family (*Asteraceae*)
Edible Chrysanthemum or *shungiku* (*Chrysanthemum coronarium*) has tender, finely dissected leaves that are plucked for salads. The young shoots are stir-fried in Asian dishes.

valerian family (*Valerianaceae*)
Corn Salad or *mâche* (*Valerianella locusta*) is a small, slow-growing, frost-tolerant plant that forms a clump of rounded, slightly fuzzy leaves. Its mild flavour doesn't become bitter when it blooms. The small plants are harvested as whole rosettes, and served in salads with their roots trimmed off.

Onion ... *For the Enthusiastic Gardener*
Allium cepa
Family: onion (*Alliaceae*)
Type: cool-season bulb

'Ailsa Craig' onions

Height: up to 60 cm (24 in.)
Space: 5 cm (2 in.) for greens, 10 cm (4 in.) or more for mature bulbs
Light: full sun; scallions tolerate partial shade
Propagation: seed outdoors in early spring; seed indoors in late February, transplant outdoors in early to mid-May; plant sets in early to mid-May
Seed Viability: retains 50% germination for 2 years

Onions appear to have arisen from a wild species in central Asia and have been cultivated for thousands of years. They were discovered in Egyptian tombs, where it was believed that the round bulb of rings symbolized eternal life.

The aroma of freshly harvested onions is enticing, and the gigantic sweet types are particularly worth the trouble, although you must keep them weeded and root maggots can be a problem. Day-length and temperature influences the development of onion bulbs; long-day cultivars are appropriate for the prairies.

How to Grow: Onions can be grown from seed, one-year-old bulbs called sets, or young transplants. The large sweet types require a long season to mature and must be planted from sets or young transplants.

Seed directly outdoors 1 cm (0.5 in.) deep as soon as the soil can be worked. Alternately, to help retain moisture, prepare a seedbed that is depressed 2.5 cm (1 in.) deeper than the surface of the surrounding soil, then press the seeds into the soil and cover them with 0.5 cm (0.25 in.) of soil. Onion sprouts emerge as a fragile green loop above the soil. Thin the seedlings to the desired spacing when the loop straightens and keep the slender seedlings weeded.

Plant sets with the top of the tiny bulb level with the surface. Sets can be purchased, or started from seed for next year's crop. To produce your own sets, sow the seed thickly so the seedlings are forced to produce tiny bulbs. Dig up the sets after the green tops have fallen and withered, and dry them in a warm, dark spot. During winter, store the sets in a plastic bag in the refrigerator and plant them the following spring.

Transplants seedlings outdoors about 5 cm (2 in.) deep. Seedlings should be started indoors about ten weeks before they can be planted outdoors, and grown using an equal day and night cycle of light.

Onions require evenly moist soil to develop good flavour. Top-dress the plants with compost to retain moisture near their shallow roots, and lightly hill soil around the base of the plants if the bulbs are pushed out of the soil as they grow. Prevent damage from the onion root maggot by installing a floating row cover at planting.

Onion leaves are hollow at the base and new leaves grow up through the tube formed at the base of older leaves. The result is a series of leaf bases in concentric rings that thicken and form the onion bulb. When the onion matures, the inner leaves do not produce new blades, so that the neck becomes hollow and flops over. Withhold irrigation at this time to allow the bulbs to dry.

Onion root maggots pose a serious threat in some areas and infested onions and onion refuse should be disposed of to prevent over-wintering sites for this pest.

Harvest: Any cultivar can be pulled when it's immature and used for green onions. Harvest bulbs during dry weather after the necks are fairly dry and the tops fall over. If the tops are bent over prematurely while the necks are thick, the bulbs are more likely to rot in storage. Lift onions with a digging fork and avoid bruising them. Cure bulbs in a single layer on newspaper in a warm, well-ventilated place out of direct sunlight for one week. Once the neck dries completely, cut the tops off the bulbs leaving a 2.5 cm (1 in.) neck and the bulb's protective papery layers intact.

Sweet onions with thick necks do not keep well. The shelf life of storage onions depends on the cultivar, the maturity of the bulb, and the storage conditions. Storage onions can be refrigerated, although they will sprout soon after being brought into room temperature. Onions can also be kept in mesh bags at room temperature for short periods, but dehydration affects their quality.

Save Seeds: Onions are cross-pollinated by insects, so it's necessary to treat them according to the instructions for saving biennials in Chapter 3, and to bag and hand-pollinate the flowers to obtain pure seed. Collect the globe-shaped flower heads when they slightly dry, and continue drying them in a paper bag to catch the dark seeds as they shatter.

Serve: Sulphur compounds are responsible for the pungent aroma and flavour that makes onions invaluable in the kitchen. These compounds also help prevent decay; strong-flavoured storage onions are high in sulphur compounds and keep better than

Japanese bunching onions

'Moss Curled' parsley

sweet types. Cutting the onion releases the sulphur compounds into the air where they form weak acids that irritate eyes. This reaction is slower when the onion is cold, and you will likely have fewer tears if you chill the onion before chopping it.

Suggested Cultivars
'Kelsae Giant' is a hybrid that produces an enormous sweet Spanish-type bulb.
'Ailsa Craig' is an open-pollinated heirloom and produces a very large, sweet bulb.
'Mars' is a hybrid red storage onion.
'Red Burgermaster' is a productive hybrid that forms large red bulbs that store well.
'Copra' is a hybrid, medium-sized, yellow storage onion.
'Southport White Globe' is a white storage onion.
'Yellow Globe Danvers' is a heritage variety that produces a large round yellow storage onion.

Related Species
Japanese Bunching Onions (*Allium fistulosum*) have hollow cylindrical leaves, but do not form bulbs. Sow seeds 0.5 cm (0.25 in.) deep in spring as soon as the ground can be worked.

The thread-like seedlings require meticulous weeding throughout the season. Some gardeners opt to hill soil around the base of the plants as they increase in girth to increase the length of the tender white portion. Bunching onions can be easily grown in containers. Harvest when the greens reach the desired size, usually about the diameter of a pencil at the base, by pulling them or lifting them with a digging fork.

Suggested Cultivars
'Kincho' is open-pollinated and has mild flavour.
'Tokyo Long White Bunching' is a disease-resistant heirloom.

Parsley
Petroselinum crispum var. *crispum* (curly type)
Petroselinum crispum var. *neapolitanum* (Italian flat-leaf type)
Family: parsley (*Apiaceae*)
Type: cool-season biennial
Height: 30 to 45 cm (12 to 18 in.)
Space: 25 to 30 cm (10 to 12 in.)
Light: full sun to part shade
Propagation: seed outdoors in early spring; seed indoors in March and transplant outdoors in mid-May
Seed Viability: Seed retains 50% germination for 3 years

Parsley ranks as the most popular cultivated herb. Originally from Europe and western Asia, its mild flavour is savoured in countless recipes, and it is a rich source of vitamin C. Many prefer the flavour of flat-leaf or Italian parsley; the curly type makes a handsome, frilly garnish. In the garden, parsley forms a clump of deep green foliage, which is a food source for caterpillars of the swallowtail butterfly.

How to Grow: Sow parsley 1 cm (0.5 in.) deep outdoors as soon as the soil can be worked, when the temperature reaches 4°C (40°F), or transplant seedlings. Darkness promotes germination, so cover the seeds completely. The seeds are notoriously slow to sprout because they contain a germination inhibitor. To accelerate germination, leach away the inhibitor by soaking the seeds for forty-eight hours before sowing them. During this soak, change and discard the water twice. Another leaching technique is to pour hot water over newly sown seeds.

   Transplants should be handled carefully to avoid disturbing the taproot, or the plant may bolt. Parsley grows well in a container.

Harvest: Pluck leaves from the outer edges of the plant as new growth arises from the centre.

Save Seeds: To save seeds, allow only one cultivar of parsley to overwinter in the garden and mulch the plants. The

Italian flat-leaf parsley

seeds develop from flat flower heads the following spring. Harvest the seed-heads as the seeds dry, and rub them off the heads.

Serve: Tied together with thyme and bay leaf, parsley becomes part of a traditional French *bouquet garni* or "garnished bundle" to flavour soup and stew. Fresh leaves are delicious in salads and dressings, and are essential to Italian tomato sauces combined with basil, oregano, and garlic.

Preserve: Parsley becomes bland when dried, but the leaves can be blanched, brushed with olive oil, and frozen between sheets of waxed paper.

Suggested Cultivars
'Moss Curled' is a popular heirloom
   variety of curly parsley from 1863.

'Hamburg Root' parsley is grown for its thickened root.

'Dark Green Italian' is an open-pollinated, flat-leaved cultivar.

Related Species

'Hamburg Root' Parsley (*Petroselinum crispum* var. *tuberosum)* is a German heirloom cultivated since before
1600. It is sown in early spring or in
late October for a crop the following
season, and produces a thick 25 cm (10
in.) taproot that is used to flavour soup,
as well as parsley-flavoured leaves.

Peas

Pisum sativum
Family: pea (*Fabaceae*)
Height: up to 2 m (6.5 ft)
Type: cool-season annual
Space: 5 cm (2 in.)

Light: full sun
Propagation: seed outdoors in early
spring
Seed Viability: seeds retain 50% germination for 3 years

Originally from the Mediterranean
area near Turkey, garden peas have
been cultivated for thousands of years.
Pea plants played a significant role in
science when the Austrian, Gregor
Mendel, crossed thousands of white
and purple-flowered varieties to study
inherited characteristics in the mid
1800s. His discoveries laid the founda-
tion for modern genetic studies.

There are three types of peas grown
for fresh eating: garden peas, snap
peas, and snow peas. Garden peas, also
known as shelling peas, have a tough
inedible pod and are cultivated for the
immature seeds inside. Snap peas were
developed in the 1970s and became
popular because they have rounded
edible pods that are less fibrous than
garden peas. Snow peas are consumed,
pod and all, while flat and unripe. Both
snap peas and snow peas are listed as
edible-pod peas in seed catalogues.

Like other legumes, peas host
beneficial bacteria that colonize their
roots and fix nitrogen from the air
into a form that plants can use. The
bacteria naturally occur in the soil,
although fertilizer inputs can dimin-
ish their numbers. A specific bacteria
associates with peas; other legumes
host other species of bacteria. Once
peas have been grown in your garden,

Developing 'Homesteader' peas

Pea vines supported on a simple trellis of stakes and twine.

the bacteria remain in the soil for some time and can colonize future pea crops. Bolstering the bacteria count with a commercially prepared powder has been shown to increase yields.

How to Grow: Sow peas 2.5 cm (1 in.) deep in early spring as soon as the soil can be worked and the temperature reaches 4°C (40°F). To inoculate the seeds with bacteria, moisten them and put them in a bag with the powder, shake to coat the seeds, and plant them immediately.

Pea vines vary in height, depending on the cultivar, but all types require some sort of support to grow on. Dwarf or determinate vines are less than 90 cm (3 ft.) and have a concen-trated pod set, while indeterminate vines reach 1.5 m (5 ft.) or more, and set pods over a longer period of time. If the plant is guided to the support, it will clasp it and continue to climb with its tendrils. Dwarf peas can be grown in containers.

Peas grow best in cool, moist conditions, and yields will be reduced if the plants experience drought or heat during flowering. Powdery mildew can be a serious problem, especially late in the growing season.

Harvest: Garden peas are ready to pick and shell when round seeds fill the pods. Snap peas are best just as the pod swells, but before the seeds grow large. Pick snow peas while the pods are still young and flat, as soon as the peas begin to form. Pull peas gently so the vine isn't damaged, and pick every few days to encourage the plant to continue producing. Immediately chill the pods after harvest. Garden peas and snap peas retain quality flavour for only two or three days, but snow peas keep two weeks. Pods left on the vine eventually turn starchy.

Save Seeds: Most peas are self-pollinating and seeds are easy to save. Snap peas are the exception, because all cultivars are hybrids. Allow the pods to dry on the vine. Shell them and continue to dry the peas indoors until the seeds shatter, rather than mash, when hit with a hammer. Store dried pea seeds in paper bags.

Serve: Peas taste best straight from the vine because their sugars convert to starch as soon as they are picked. They are delicious fresh or lightly steamed. Snow peas are a classic component of stir-fries. The young leafy shoots of snow peas are also a delicacy for salads or stir-fries.

Preserve: Peas and snow pea pods retain good flavour if they are frozen within a couple hours of picking. Before freezing, blanch them briefly.

Suggested Cultivars
Garden pea, shelling type
'Bolero' is open-pollinated, productive, and very disease-resistant.

'Green Arrow' is a popular open-pollinated cultivar that produces on long vines.

'Homesteader' (also known as 'Lincoln') is a popular heirloom that produces on short vines and withstands heat.

'Little Marvel' is an early heirloom that produces on dwarf vines and is suitable for container growing.

Snap pea, edible pod
'Cascadia' is a productive hybrid with short, disease-resistant vines.

Snow pea, edible pod
'Dwarf Grey Sugar' is an early-maturing heirloom that produces on dwarf vines with attractive rosy-purple flowers.

'Oregon Sugar Pod' is open-pollinated, white-flowered, and produces quality peas on short vines.

Potato
Solanum tuberosum ssp. *tuberosum*
Family: nightshade (*Solanaceae*)
Type: cool-season annual
Height: up to 60 cm (2 ft.)
Space: 30 cm (12 in.) for early cultivars, 45 cm (18 in.) for mid-season and late cultivars
Light: Full sun
Propagation: plant certified seed potatoes outdoors in early to mid-May

Potatoes are the fourth largest food crop in the world, after rice, wheat, and corn. There are about five thousand cultivated varieties, and over half of these are grown in the Andes region

Potatoes can be grown in a raised bed.   'Norland' potatoes

of South America, where the potato originated. Potatoes grown in North America and Europe belong to a single species that is adapted to cool weather and long days. A serious fungal disease wiped out cultivars of the same species during the Great Irish Famine, which began in 1845.

Some factors to consider when choosing potato cultivars are storage capability, disease resistance, and use. Early-maturing cultivars yield the first new potatoes and form the most compact plants. Late-maturing varieties form large plants with sprawling foliage and produce the best storage tubers. Cultivar descriptions often indicate whether the potato is best boiled, baked, or fried.

All green parts of the potato plant contain toxic compounds. Tubers can accumulate these compounds also, and the amount increases with exposure to sunlight. Any green patches on a potato should be cut off and not consumed; the remainder of the tuber is fine to eat.

How to Grow: It's important to plant certified seed potatoes because many diseases affect potatoes. Tubers from the grocery store can carry disease without showing symptoms. Seed potatoes are not true seeds, but are actually disease-free potatoes that were produced the previous year specifically for planting.

Plant seed potatoes when soil temperatures reach at least 8°C (46°F), as they can rot in lower soil temperatures. Small seed potatoes, 2.5 to 5 cm (1 to 2 in.) in diameter, are optimum for planting and yield better than cut potatoes. Larger potatoes should be cut into pieces with two to three eyes, and allowed to dry at room temperature two days before planting. Plant the seed potato 5 cm (2 in.) deep, and hill soil around the base of the plant as it grows, until it is buried 20 to 30 cm (8 to 12 in.) deep to protect the tubers from light.

Compact, early-season potato cultivars can be grown in very large containers, such as plastic tubs or garbage cans with holes cut in the bottom for drainage.

Irrigate potato plants from the time the first shoots emerge until September, when water should be withheld to allow the plants to die back. Watch for the black-and-yellow-striped Colorado potato beetle, as infestations can defoliate potato plants entirely. Hand-pick the beetles and their orange eggs that are found on the underside of leaves.

Scab is a bacterial disease that appears as dark lesions on the potato skin, but it is merely cosmetic and doesn't affect flavour or yield. Some cultivars are more susceptible to scab, but it can be simply removed by peeling the potato before preparing it.

Harvest: Tubers begin forming around the time flower buds appear. Probe the base of the plant to check the size. Immature or "new" potatoes are harvested by hand when they reach 2.5 to 5 cm (1 to 2 in.). Larger potatoes can be dug during the season for immediate consumption. Mature potatoes should be left in the ground for one to two weeks after the vines die back, in order to develop thick skins so that they will store well. Remove the vines if they don't naturally wither or get hit by frost. The tubers will tolerate frost, but not a hard freeze, and should be dug before temperatures drop below minus 3°C (27°F). Insert a digging fork about 30 cm (12 in.) from the centre of the plant, lift it, and separate the potatoes

from the roots. Handle the potatoes gently to avoid bruising them. Speared potatoes cannot be stored.

Cure the potatoes in a cool 15°C (59°F), dark place for several days and gently brush off the soil, but do not wash the tubers before storing them. Small quantities of potatoes can be stored at room temperature, but they will eventually sprout. Potatoes are naturally dormant for about two months; after that they must be stored in the dark, with temperatures between 5°C to 10°C (41°F to 50°F) to prevent sprouting, and with plenty of humidity to reduce shrinking from dehydration.

Traditionally, potatoes were stored in root cellars. A contemporary compromise is to store them in perforated plastic bags in an unheated area of the home where they will not freeze, such as a basement. Home refrigerators are usually too cool, causing the starch in potatoes to convert to sugar, and giving them a sweet off-taste. Stored potatoes should be checked frequently for signs of rot.

Serve: Tender new potatoes are a special treat, steamed and tossed with butter and a snippet of dill, parsley, or chives.

Suggested Cultivars
Early
'Norland' is a popular compact, disease-resistant, red-skinned potato that is good for boiling and

the earliest new potatoes. It's possible to plant this cultivar in late June to produce a fall crop of small new potatoes.

Mid-season

'AC Peregrine' was registered in 2000, after being selected in Lethbridge, Alberta, for prairie conditions. It has red skin and white flesh and is disease-resistant and good for boiling and new potatoes.

'Pontiac' is a red-skinned variety that tolerates heavy soil, but is susceptible to scab disease. It produces large potatoes that are good for boiling.

'Purple Viking' is a mid-season novelty cultivar with purple skin and white flesh.

'Yukon Gold' is a popular, productive, yellow-fleshed all-purpose potato.

Late

'All Red' is a novelty cultivar with red skin and pinkish-red flesh.

'Banana' produces small fingerling all-purpose potatoes with yellow skin and waxy yellow flesh.

'Bintje' has yellow skin and yellow flesh that is best for boiling, but it can also be baked or fried.

'Russian Blue' is a novelty variety with violet skin and brilliant purple flesh, recommended for roasting or grilling.

Radish

Raphanus sativus
Family: mustard (Brassicaceae)
Type: cool-season annual
Height: 7 to 13 cm (3 to 5 in.)
Space: 5 cm (2 in.)
Light: full sun

Assorted radish cultivars

Propagation: seed outdoors in early spring
Seed Viability: 5 years

Radishes, as we know them, were probably domesticated a few thousand years ago in west Asia and Europe. In Asia, the 50 cm (20 in.) daikon radish was developed, and in India, radishes have been selected for 30 cm (12 in.) seedpods that are used in curries and pickles. The garden radish is grown mostly for its thick, short taproot, although the greens can be cooked and the flowers and seedpods make interesting salad additions.

How to Grow: Sow radish seeds 1 cm (0.5 in.) deep outdoors as soon as the soil can be worked and the soil temperature reaches 4°C (40°F). Plant small amounts every couple weeks for an extended harvest. Make a final sowing in mid-August for a fall crop. Radishes can be grown in containers.

Radishes bolt as the days become long, regardless of temperature. Like other mustard family relatives, radishes attract pests such as flea beetles and root maggots, and are sometimes even used as a fast-growing "trap crop" in organic gardens to lure the pests away from other crops. Floating row covers can block infestations from these insects.

Harvest: Radishes grow very quickly and mature within a month after sowing. Probe the soil to see if the roots have reached their mature size and pull them when they are less than 2.5 cm (1 in.) in diameter.

Save Seeds: Radishes are cross-pollinated by insects and can cross with turnips, rutabagas, mustard, and Chinese cabbages. The flowering stalk is 90 cm (3 ft.) tall; seeds are ripe when the pods dry on the stalk, and the hard pods can be split with a hammer.

Serve: Sulphur chemicals give radishes their sharp, spicy bite. Thin slices of fresh, crisp roots will liven up a salad.

Suggested Cultivars

'Cherry Belle' is a 1949 heirloom that produces a round, red 2.5 cm (1 in.) root.
'Champion' is an open-pollinated, deep red round root that is heat-resistant.
'Easter Egg' is open-pollinated and produces a small round root in shades of red, white, or purple.
'French Breakfast' is a popular heirloom from 1879 that produces a 5 cm (2 in.) red root tipped in white.
'Sparkler' is an heirloom variety and a classic radish: round and red with a white tip.
'White Icicle' is an heirloom variety that produces a pure white 12.5 cm (5 in.) long root.

Related Species ... For the Enthusiastic Gardener

Turnips (*Brassica rapa*) and Rutabagas (*Brassica napus*) are biennial cool-

Rutabagas   Turnips

season crops that are cultivated for their swollen underground structures. Both are grown in a similar manner to radishes, only they require a longer season to mature, and often suffer significant damage from flea beetles and root maggots. Floating row covers help prevent insect infestations.

Seed turnips and rutabagas 1 cm (0.5 in.) deep outdoors in early May. Thin turnips 5 to 10 cm (2 to 4 in.) apart, and thin rutabagas 15 cm (6 in.) apart. Turnip greens are harvested for salads or cooked greens when they are 7.5 to 10 cm (3 to 4 in.) long. Pull turnips when they reach 5 to 7.5 cm (2 to 3 in.) in diameter, and harvest rutabagas when they reach 7 to 12 cm (3 to 5 in.) in diameter. Remove the tops and refrigerate unwashed turnips and rutabagas. Wash and dry turnip greens before refrigerating them.

Suggested Cultivars
Rutabaga
'Laurentian' is an heirloom with a pale

yellow root and a purple neck.
Turnip
'Purple Top White Globe' is an heirloom that forms a round purple and white root.

Shallots
Allium cepa var. *aggregatum*
Family: onion (*Allliaceae*)
Type: cool-season bulb
Height: 30 cm (12 in.)
Space: 15 cm (6 in.)
Light: full sun or partial shade
Propagation: plant bulb in early spring

Shallots are a type of onion that forms a clump of multiple pointed bulbs with tubular leaves. Technically, shallots and multiplier onions are the same plant, but those with copper skins are known as shallots, and those with yellow or brown skins are usually referred to as multiplier onions. Shallots are thought to have a sweeter, milder flavour. The British are known to have cultivated

Shallots

shallots since the early 1700s, and the bulb was likely grown in France as early as the twelfth century.

How to Grow: Although they are considered a gourmet member of the onion family, shallots are easy to cultivate in the garden or in containers. They are usually planted from one-year-old bulbs called sets, as soon as the soil can be worked in early spring. Place each bulb 2 to 5 cm (1 to 2 in.) deep, such that the pointed end is up and the tip is level with the soil surface. Allow 15 cm (6 in.) between planted bulbs, as each one will produce a cluster of new bulbs.

The plants are shallow-rooted and require evenly moist soil throughout the growing season. As they grow, the bulb clusters will emerge aboveground.

Shallots are hardy and will likely survive winter to produce very early greens the following spring, if the plants are mulched.

Harvest: Cut or pull less than one-third of the greens when they are 15 to 20 cm (6 to 8 in.) long. Leave the remaining greens to produce food for the developing bulbs. Lift the bulbs as the tops yellow and begin to die back in mid to late summer. Cure the bulbs by spreading them out on newspapers in a well-ventilated place, out of direct light, to dry for two weeks.

Store shallots for a few weeks in clusters in a mesh or paper bag or a wire basket in a cool, dark place, and break the clusters apart just before use. To prevent sprouting during longer storage, refrigerate them.

Save Seeds: Store some of the largest

'Bloomsdale Longstanding' spinach

bulbs from your crop for planting the following spring. The plants will flower and produce seed the second year, but shallots are propagated more quickly from bulbs.

Serve: Shallots develop their characteristic delicate flavour when sautéed lightly in butter or roasted. The bulbs can be substituted for onions in any recipe and are particularly good in sauces. The bulbs are easier to peel after they are blanched: drop them in boiling water for twenty seconds and rinse them in cool water. Use sliced shallot greens to add a hint of onion to salads or dressings.

Spinach
Spinacia oleracea
Family: goosefoot (*Chenopodiaceae*)
Type: cool-season annual

Space: 10 to 15 cm (4 to 6 in.)
Light: full sun to part shade
Propagation: seed outdoors in early spring
Seed Viability: 5 years

Spinach originates from southwest Asia, and is related to beets and chard. The savoy type with crinkly leaves is popular because it contains lower amounts of oxalic acid, which gives the leaves their tangy bite. Smooth-leaved spinach has a higher concentration of oxalic acid, grows faster, yields more, and is used for commercial processing. In addition to true spinach, many gardeners grow a similar, but botanically unrelated warm-season plant from New Zealand known as New Zealand spinach (*Tetragonia tetragonioides*), which is planted outdoors after the frost date and produces well in summer heat.

How to Grow: Seed spinach 0.5 cm (0.25 in.) deep outdoors as early as the soil can be worked and the soil temperature reaches 4°C (40°F). Spinach will bolt in response to long days, even when the plants are still small. Flowering is accelerated when the weather is hot or the plants are crowded.

Harvest: Begin cutting baby spinach when the plant has at least six leaves, removing the outer leaves first. Harvesting the largest and oldest leaves every few days can delay flowering slightly, by interrupting the chemical signal that causes flowering, since it is transported from the leaves to the growing point of the plant. As soon as the central flowering stalk begins to appear, harvest the entire plant by cutting it off just above the soil surface.

Save Seeds: It's very difficult to save pure strains of spinach seed because male and female flowers are on different plants, and its fine pollen is transported long distances by wind.

Serve: Fresh, steamed, or sautéed spinach adds robust flavour to salads, quiche, soups, and dips. Combined with feta cheese, it makes up the filling for *spanakopita*, a Greek savoury pastry.

Preserve: Blanch and freeze spinach leaves.

Suggested Cultivars

'Bloomsdale Longstanding' is an heirloom savoy type with deeply crinkled leaves.

'Skookum' is a hybrid, bolt-resistant, semi-savoy type that is productive and disease-resistant.

'Tyee' is an early-maturing, bolt-resistant, disease-resistant hybrid, semi-savoy type with lightly crinkled leaves.

Related Species

Orach (*Atriplex hortensis*) is a cool-season annual that is grown for its leaves, which make a good fresh or cooked substitute for spinach or chard. Seed orach outdoors 0.5 cm (0.25 in.) deep as soon as the ground can be worked in spring, in a site with full sun. Thin the seedlings 5 cm (2 in.) apart. Harvest young plants when they reach 10 to 15 cm (4 to 6 in.) or pick young leaves of mature plants. If left to flower, the plant grows to 1 to 1.5m (3 to 5 ft.). Green orach tastes mild, but the ruby red type is more ornamental.

Orach

Quinoa (*Chenopodium quinoa*) is a cool-season annual grown for its nutritious seeds that are consumed like a grain. Seed quinoa 0.5 cm (0.25 in.) deep outdoors in full sun as soon as the soil can be worked in spring. Thin the seedlings to 5 cm (2 in.) apart, and thin progressively to a final spacing of 30 cm (12 in.) apart. Quinoa seedlings look similar to lambsquarters (*Chenopodium album*), a weedy cousin that is also edible. Quinoa grows 1 to 2 m (1 to 2 yd.) tall.

Harvest by cutting the ripe seed heads from the stalk after the stems become dry and leafless, before the first fall frost. To separate and clean the seeds, rub them from the seedhead into a container, pass them through a screen, and lightly blow off any remaining bits of dried leaves. Be sure the seed is thoroughly dried and store it in an airtight container in a cool, dry place.

Before consuming quinoa, it should be soaked and rinsed to remove the soapy seed coating. Soak it twice for two hours, rinsing it through a strainer after each soak. Prepare quinoa by bringing one cup of grain and two cups of water to a boil, and cover and simmer it for fifteen minutes; fluff cooked quinoa with a fork.

Warm-season Vegetables and Herbs
Artichoke, Globe ... *For the Enthusiastic Gardener*
Cynara cardunculus
Family: sunflower (*Asteraceae*)
Type: cool-season tender perennial grown as an annual
Height: 1 to 1.2 m (3 to 4 ft.)
Space: 1 m (3 ft.)
Light: full sun
Propagation: seed indoors in mid-February, transplant outdoors after the frost date
Seed Viability: 1 year

Mediterranean in origin, globe artichokes were prized by the Greeks and Romans and were first cultivated for medicinal purposes. Enormous immature flower buds are the edible portion of this large, dramatic plant

ROASTED ROOT RECIPE

Roasting concentrates the sweetness of root crops like potatoes, carrots, celeriac, beets, and parsnips. Prepare roots by scrubbing them and cut them into 2.5 cm (1 in.) pieces. Drizzle 15 to 30 ml (1 to 2 Tbsp.) of canola or olive oil over the pieces and toss them so they are lightly coated. Season them with salt, pepper, or dried herbs. Roast for forty minutes in a 200°C (400°F) oven, stirring occasionally, until the vegetables are tender and golden brown around the edges.

Globe artichokes

with arching silver leaves. If left to open, the buds reveal purple thistle-like flowers. Artichokes are perennial plants in warm climates, but some cultivars can be coaxed to produce the same year from seed in short-season gardens.

How to grow: Sow artichokes 0.5 cm (0.25 in.) deep indoors 12 weeks before the frost date. Germination takes two to three weeks at room temperature; bottom heat of 25°C (77°F) accelerates sprouting. Discard any pale-coloured seedlings, and transplant the largest plants to 10 cm (4 in.) individual pots and grow them at room temperature with cool nights of 10°C to 15°C (50°F to 60°F). The artichoke requires a chilling period of at least 250 hours or more than ten days

below (10°C) 50°F to induce flower buds, but the plants are not frost-tolerant. Expose the potted plants to chilling as spring weather permits, and protect them or bring them indoors when frost is forecast. Transplant the seedlings outdoors as soon as the danger of frost is over.

Harvest: Cut immature flower buds when they reach 7.5 to 10 cm (3 to 4 in.) while they are green and tight.

Serve: To prepare, trim the stem off just below the artichoke bud, cut 1 to 2.5 cm (0.5 to 1 in.) off the top, and rub the cut surfaces with lemon to prevent discoloration. Steam the entire bud until tender (the outer leaves should pull away from the bud easily), usually thirty to forty-five minutes. To eat, pull off individual leafy bracts, dip them in butter and lemon or vinaigrette, strip the fleshy inside off with your teeth and discard the leathery bract. Once the stringy centre is reached, discard the fibres and scoop out the edible fleshy heart at the base.

Suggested Cultivar
'Imperial Star' is an early-maturing hybrid, developed specifically for cultivation as an annual, at the University of California at Davis.

Basil
Ocimum basilicum
Family: mint (*Lamiaceae*)
Type: warm-season annual

Height: 30 to 40 cm (12 to 16 in.)
Space: 20 to 25 cm (8 to 10 in.)
Light: full sun
Propagation: seed indoors in early April, transplant outdoors in early June; seed outdoors after frost date
Seed Viability: 5 years

Heat-loving basil comes from India and tropical Asia, where it has been cultivated as a seasoning for thousands of years. Named after the Greek *basileus* for "king," the herb also reigns in Italy and was incorporated into that regional cuisine centuries ago. Between an assortment of Asian and Mediterranean cultivars, basil exudes scents from the same chemicals found in lemon peel, anise, cinnamon, geranium, coriander, tarragon, bay, pine, and cloves.

How to grow: Sow basil indoors six weeks before the frost date, pressing the seeds into the soil and barely covering them, and warm the soil with bottom heat to prevent damping off. Transplant seedlings outdoors when the soil temperature is at least 18°C (65°F). Seeds can also be sown directly outdoors at this time.

As the seedlings develop three pairs of leaves, pinch them back to just above the first pair to encourage branching. It is essential to grow basil in full sun and well-drained soil, and it's the ideal container plant for a hot location. It grows rapidly in hot weather, but during chilly spells, growth stalls and the plant may bolt. In places where cool weather is common, basil grows better under a cold frame.

Harvest: Pick leaves or clip leafy stems just before use. Cut the stems back to two pairs of leaves to encourage branching and delay flowering. Once flowers develop, leaf production slows and the essential oils decline.

Store unwashed leafy stems for a few days in a glass of water at room temperature, changing the water daily.

Save Seeds: Allow basil to bloom; as the bottom seed capsules turn brown, cut the stalk and dry it in a paper bag. Rub the capsules on a screen to separate the dry bits from the dark seeds.

Serve: Basil is sensitive to chilling and bruises easily. To prevent dark blotches on the leaves, handle them gently, rinse them with lukewarm water, and use a salad spinner to dry them.

Basil and tomato are perfect partners chopped fresh or in pasta sauce.

'Purple Ruffles' and 'Genovese' basil

Basil is the main ingredient of Italian *pesto*, a rich paste prepared with olive oil, garlic, pine nuts, and Parmesan cheese.

Preserve: The best way to preserve basil is frozen in pesto. Basil leaves can also be blanched on the stem, brushed with olive oil and packed between sheets of waxed paper in airtight containers and frozen. Frozen basil turns brown and mushy when it thaws, so add it to soups and sauces straight from the freezer. Dried basil has greatly diminished flavour.

Suggested Cultivars

'Genovese' is an open-pollinated, large-leaved cultivar that is ideal for pesto.

'Martina' is open-pollinated, slow to bolt, and similar to 'Genovese.'

'Mrs. Burns' is an heirloom with a citrus fragrance.

'Purple Ruffles' hybrid has striking deep purple foliage with ruffled leaf margins that is useful as an accent plant and to make herbal vinegar.

'Red Rubin' is a slow-growing hybrid that reliably produces dark red-violet foliage.

'Siam Queen' is a hybrid with dark green leaves and showy burgundy flowering stalks, used in Thai cooking.

'Spicy Globe' is a hybrid that forms a dwarf mound of tiny leaves and makes an attractive container or edging plant.

Beans, Common

Phaseolus vulgaris
Family: bean (*Fabaceae*)
Type: warm-season annual
Height: bush (determinate) 30 cm (12 in.); vine (indeterminate) up to 2.4 m (8 ft.)
Space: bush 20 cm (8 in.); vine 15 cm (6 in.); dry beans 45 cm (18 in.)
Light: full sun
Propagation: seed outdoors after the frost date
Seed Viability: retains 50% germination for 4 years

Most common bean varieties originate in the Americas, and have been cultivated for over six thousand years. The bean family is one of the largest plant groups in the world, and is the second most important food family after the grass family, which includes grains. Beans and grains contain complementary proteins, and when eaten together they can provide a complete source of essential proteins.

Common green beans and wax beans are consumed as immature seedpods; wax beans differ in that their seedpods turn yellow as they lengthen. Dry beans or soup beans are harvested after the seeds fill the pod and dry on the vine, which requires a long growing season.

Beans have the ability to host certain bacteria in nodules on their roots. The bacteria convert nitrogen from the air that is trapped in soil pores into a form that the plant can use, and

Determinate bush beans like 'Royal Burgundy' are compact and self-supporting.

Indeterminate pole beans require a vertical support.

the bean plant supplies food to the bacteria in return. These bacteria occur naturally in the soil, and once beans are cultivated in your garden, it's likely they will be there to colonize future bean crops. It's also possible to bolster the nitrogen-fixing activity by coating your beans with a commercially prepared bacteria powder.

There are two types of bean plants: determinate bush beans and indeterminate pole (vine) beans. Bush beans form compact plants that stop growing when flower buds develop, and produce a single crop of beans that ripens within a short period. Bush beans produce earlier than pole beans, and gardeners often make more than one sowing to extend the bush bean harvest.

Pole beans initially devote energy to growing vines, which climb by coiling counter-clockwise up poles, strings or other plants. Pole beans begin producing later than bush beans, but they produce until frost, so only one crop is sown. Supported pole beans are more productive in a small space than bush beans.

How to Grow: Sow beans outdoors after the frost date when the soil warms to at least 15°C (60°F). Seed them 2.5 cm (1 in.) deep and 5 to 7.5 cm (2 to 3 in.) apart. To inoculate your beans with commercial bacteria powder, moisten the seeds, put them in a bag with the bacteria and shake to coat the seeds. Plant the seeds immediately, before the coating dries. Bush beans are self-supporting, but pole beans should be sown at the base of a support.

A bean tipi is a popular support, made by lashing three poles together at the top to form a tripod. The poles should be 1.8 to 2.7 m (6 to 9 ft.) long, spaced 60 to 90 cm. (2 to 3 ft.) apart at the base, and set into the ground 30 to 45 cm (12 to 18 in.) deep.

Thin the seedlings when they are 30 cm (6 in.) tall to the appropriate spacing for the cultivar, removing those that are different in size or leaf appearance. Beans are shallow-rooted and should be weeded by hand, rather than with a hoe. Maintain consistent moisture during blossoming to prevent flower drop, but avoid harvesting and weeding when the plants are wet to prevent disease problems.

Harvest: Harvest green beans when they form smooth, slim pods, about the diameter of a pencil. To encourage continuous pole bean production, pick every few days. Pick dry beans at the end of the season when the pods are completely dry. Shell the pods and store dry beans in a paper bag, not in an airtight container.

Save Seeds: Beans self-pollinate, although insects can cross-pollinate them within close range. Allow the pods to dry on the plant. If frost is predicted when the pods are nearly mature, pull the entire plant and hang it upside down in a warm place where the seeds can draw energy from the plant a few days longer. Shell the seeds and if they shatter rather than squish when hit with a hammer, they are sufficiently dry to store in paper envelopes or bags.

Serve: Simply snap off the stem end of green beans and steam them for three minutes or until tender before serving.

Preserve: Blanch beans and freeze them.

Suggested Cultivars
Bush (determinate)
'Gold Rush' is an open-pollinated yellow wax bean.
'Hutterite Soup' is an early-maturing heirloom dry bean. It is yellow-green with a dark ring around the eye and is excellent for making soup.
'Nickel' is open-pollinated and produces green, thin, French-filet type pods.
'Pencil Pod Black Wax' is a 1900 heirloom with yellow pods.
'Provider' is an early-maturing, productive, open-pollinated green bean.
'Royal Burgundy' is open-pollinated and bears dark purple pods that become green when cooked.
'Venture' is an open-pollinated, prolific green bean.
Pole (indeterminate):
'Blue Lake' is a popular, open-pollinated green bean. The cultivar is also available as a determinant plant.

Unlike most beans, broad beans are a cool-season crop.

Edamame soybeans

'Kentucky Wonder' is a popular American heirloom green bean from the 1850's.

'Trionfo Violetto' is a beautiful Italian heirloom with purple pods and lavender flowers.

Related Species

Broad Bean or fava bean (*Vicia faba*) is an old world species that was grown in ancient cultures in the Mediterranean and the Middle East. Unlike common beans, broad beans are a cool-season crop that should be planted when the soil warms to 10°C (50°F), usually in early May. Sow seeds 2.5 cm (1 in.) deep and 7.5 cm (3 in.) apart, and thin the seedlings to 15 cm (6 in.) apart. Broad beans are taller than bush beans, but shorter than pole beans, and produce substantial vines up to 91 cm (36 in.) long, which require hilling or a trellis to prevent them from falling over. Pinch off the top of the plant if aphids congregate on the tips. Broad bean flowers are self-pollinating or cross-pollinated by bees. The beans ripen from the base of the stalk up, and can be picked at the desired stage, usually when the seeds fill the pod. Young leaves are edible and are used in salads or stir-fries. Preserve broad beans by shelling and blanching them before freezing. Save seeds from beans that mature until dry on the vine.

Suggested Cultivar

'Broad Windsor' is a popular English
heirloom grown since 1860.

Edamame Beans (*Glycine max*)
translated from Japanese as "beans
on branches," are immature green
soybeans from Asia that have become
a popular snack. These require a
long growing season, so choose early
maturing varieties to get a crop on the
prairies. Seed 2.5 cm (1 in.) deep and
7.5 cm (3 in.) apart in late May, and
thin to 15 cm (6 in.) apart. The plants
reach 60 cm (2 ft.). Harvest the pods
when they are light green, with two or
more seeds, and the seeds have swollen
but not quite filled the pod. Process
the pods immediately as they deteriorate by the next day. Steam the pods
until tender, pop the seeds out of the
pods, salt the seeds and pop them in
your mouth!

Suggested Cultivars

'Early Hakucho' is an early-maturing
hybrid that produces on dwarf 30
cm (1 ft.) plants.
'Envy' is an early-maturing hybrid that
was developed at the University of
New Hampshire. It produces on 60
cm (2 ft.) plants.

Runner Bean, or scarlet runner bean
(*Phaseolus coccineus*), native to Central
America, is a scarlet-flowered vine
with edible beans. Some cultivars are
white-flowered, others have sunset-
coloured blossoms. The seedling of a

'Scarlet Runner' bean vines supported by a tipi.

runner bean looks different from that
of a garden bean, because its cotyledons, or seed leaves, remain below the
ground when it germinates. The vine
climbs by twisting around any support in a clockwise direction, instead
of counter-clockwise like common
pole beans, and if you guide the stem
in the wrong direction, it may snap
off. This species is better adapted to
cool weather than common beans,
although it should be seeded at the
same time. Harvest runner beans
when they are very slender and prepare them by steaming until tender.
Runner beans are often cross-pollinated by insects or hummingbirds.
Mature, dry seeds are black mottled
with pink, and can be saved for planting the next season.

Corn must be planted in a block for effective pollination.

Suggested Cultivar:

'Scarlet Runner' is a popular heirloom from the 1700s, with bright red blossoms.

Corn … For the Enthusiastic Gardener

Zea mays
Family: grass (*Poaceae*)
Type: warm-season annual
Propagate: seed outdoors when soil temperature reaches 15°C (60°F); seed supersweet cultivars when soil temperature reaches 18°C (65°F)
Space: 20 to 30 cm (8 to 12 in.) between plants and 76 cm (30 in.) between rows
Light: full sun
Seed Viability: 1 to 2 years

Simply put, sweet corn is a giant grass that produces delicious, succulent seeds. Corn was domesticated from an ancient wild grain in southern Mexico called *teosinte*. During cultivation throughout the Americas for its starchy, dry seeds, many types and colours evolved. Sweet corn arose from field corn, through a natural mutation that nearly doubled the sugar content of the kernels.

Three main types of sweet corn are available to home gardeners. The standard sweet corn varieties (labeled *su* for "sugary") rapidly become starchy after harvest and should be eaten shortly after they are picked. A group of cultivars known as *se* for "sugar enhanced" has tender kernels that remain sweet for two to four days

Sweet corn

after harvest, if refrigerated. Super-sweet varieties (indentified as *sh2* for "shrunken") are so sugary that the kernels become shrivelled or shrunken when dry, due to lack of starch, and stay sweet up to ten days in the refrigerator. New synergistic hybrids feature different combinations of *su, se,* and *sh2* kernels on the same cob.

How to Grow: Choose early or mid–season cultivars with maturity dates of less than 80 days. Kernels function as seeds, and sweeter kernels have less starch to nourish the seedling, so *sh2* cultivars have lower germination rates and are more sensitive to cold, wet soils than the *su* and *se* cultivars. A soil thermometer is necessary to determine when to plant, as the soil temperature must reach at least 15°C (60°F) before planting *su* and *se* cultivars, and 18°C (65°F) before *sh2* cultivars are planted. Generally this occurs in late May to early June.

Corn is wind-pollinated and must be planted in blocks for effective pollination. The block should have at least four 10' rows, spaced about 76 cm (30 in.) apart, with a minimum of ten plants in each row. Sow the seeds 2.5 cm (1 in.) deep, 10 cm (4 in.) apart in the rows. To accelerate germination, cover your planting with clear plastic polyethylene sheets until germination occurs. An alternate method that allows the seedlings to develop longer under plastic is to create shallow trenches in your block, 10 cm (4 in.) deep, and plant the seeds in the trench, covering them with 2.5 cm (1 in.) of soil. Cover the trench or entire block with clear plastic mulch, and remove it after the seedlings sprout, as they reach the plastic.

Thin corn seedlings and apply a 1 cm (0.5 in.) layer of compost mulch when the plants are 12 inches high. Allow suckers that sprout near the base of the plant to grow.

The tassel at the top of the plant is a cluster of male flowers, laden with tiny pollen grains. Summer breezes shake the tassel, causing the pollen grains to shower down on the fine tufts of silks, which emerge from the tightly wrapped green cob of female flowers. Each silk strand is associated with a single kernel that must be pollinated to develop. Incomplete pollination results in ears that are partially filled.

All types of sweet corn should be isolated from popcorn or field corn to prevent starchiness. In windy areas, the pollen can be transported long distances. In addition, *sh2* cultivars must also be isolated from *su* and *se* cultivars or the *sh2* type will develop hard, starchy kernels.

Resist the temptation to create a "three sisters" garden of bean vines supported on cornstalks with squash underfoot, as it will compromise the quality and maturity of all three crops. Warm-season crops can be marginal on the prairies to begin with, and this historical planting technique isn't suitable for sweet corn.

Harvest: Sweet corn is ripe when the kernels are plump and exude a milky, rather than clear juice when punctured with a fingernail. Other signs are full, rounded ears and brown silks. Harvest by twisting the ear downwards off the stalk with one hand while holding the stalk with the other hand. Each stalk produces one to two ears. Immediately after harvesting, refrigerate the ears in their husks. Seed-saving isn't practical; there isn't enough space in a home garden to obtain the diversity needed for strong corn seeds.

Serve: To prepare, remove the husks and drop corn in boiling water for 3-5

minutes. Enjoy with butter, salt, and pepper.

Preserve: Blanch corn on the cob for 4 minutes, then cut off the kernels and freeze them.

Suggested Cultivars
Standard (su)
'Earlivee' is a very early-maturing hybrid with small cobs and yellow kernels.
'Seneca Horizon' is a productive, early hybrid with yellow kernels.
Sugar enhanced (se)
'Seneca Tomahawk' is a productive, early hybrid with yellow and white kernels.
Supersweet (sh2)
'Northern Xtra Sweet' is an early supersweet hybrid with large cobs of yellow and white kernels.
'Northern Xtra Sweet Yellow' is an early supersweet hybrid with yellow kernels.
'Vision' is a mid-season supersweet hybrid with large cobs and yellow kernels.

Cucumber
Cucumis sativus
Family: gourd (*Cucurbitaceae*)
Type: warm-season annual
Height: vine
Space: trellis-grown vine 30 cm (12 in.), bush 1 m (1 yd.)
Light: full sun
Propagation: seed indoors in early to mid-May, transplant outdoors in early

June; seed outdoors in late May to
early June
Seed Viability: 5 yrs

Cucumbers were likely domesticated
long ago in India from a wild species
in the Himalayan foothills. The vines
produce separate male and female
flowers, and pollen is transferred
between them by bees. Female flowers
can be recognized by swellings that
resemble tiny cucumbers at the base
of the flower; males have none. Many
modern cucumbers have been bred to
produce more female flowers in order
to increase yields, but these require
special steps to produce fruit. Before
choosing cultivars for your garden, it's
important to understand the differ-
ences between these three groups:
monoecious, gynoecious, and parthenocarpic.

'Straight 8' cucumbers supported on a chicken
wire trellis.

Most cucumbers are "monoecious,"
literally meaning "one house"; male
and female flowers are produced on
the same plant. Male flowers appear
first to attract pollinators, and female
flowers follow shortly. Daylength and
temperature influence flowering, and
the number of female flowers increases
in the latter part of the growing season
as days grow shorter.

Certain new hybrids, known
as "gynoecious," produce only (or
mostly) female flowers. These can bear
more fruit on a vine, but only if they
are pollinated by male flowers from
a monoecious plant. Seeds of gynoecious cultivars are usually sold with
some seeds of a monoecious cultivar
(also called males or pollinator plants
in seed catalogues) that is typically
coated with a coloured dust for identification.

A third type, often called the English cucumber, is "parthenocarpic" and
produces seedless cucumbers without
pollination. It must be isolated from
standard cucumbers and is intended
for greenhouse production.

Gardeners usually grow long cucumbers for slicing and short, blocky
ones for pickling, although many cultivars can be used for either purpose.
A mild-tasting cucumber that is bred
to have thin skin is often described as
"burpless."

Curly tendrils help cucumber vines cling to a trellis.

How to grow: Cucumbers grown from transplants are usually earlier and more productive than those that are sown directly in the garden. Before planting, warm the soil with plastic mulch. Traditionally, cucumbers are planted on low, flat mounds, about 1 m (3 ft.) wide, with three rambling vines per hill. They can also be grown on a trellis or in a large pot. Bush types are usually selected for containers. Vine types that are grown on a trellis save space, receive more sunshine and better air circulation, and produce clean, straight cucumbers. Vines cling to the trellis with tendrils and can climb it if you initially tie them up with flexible strips, like pieces of nylon stocking. Avoid locating the trellis in an exposed, windy location.

Seed indoors, 1 cm (0.5 in.) deep in individual 7.5 cm (3 in.) pots, three weeks before you plan to set them outdoors. Plant the seed with the pointed end up to help the seedling push the seed coat off as it sprouts. If the cultivar is gynoecious, sow (and label) the specially marked male seed. One plant with male flowers is sufficient to pollinate the female flowers on three plants.

Transplant seedlings that have one or two leaves outdoors after the danger of frost has passed, and the soil has warmed to 15°C (60°F). Handle the taproot carefully during transplanting. Plastic mulch and supported crop covers can be used to retain heat. Install collars around each plant to prevent cutworm damage.

Direct seeding outdoors avoids potential root damage from transplanting. After the frost date, when the soil temperature is at least 15°C (60°F), sow vine types 15 cm (6 in.) apart, and thin them to 30 cm (12 in.) apart after germination. Sow two seeds of bush types on a small mound and thin to the strongest seedling. For extra warmth and earlier production, the seeds can be sown through holes cut in black plastic mulch.

Bitterness is a genetic trait, but cool temperatures or dry soil can amplify it. Cucumbers are bee-pollinated, and cool, wet weather results in poor pollination and misshapen fruit. You can improve fruit set by transferring pollen from male flowers to females (distinguished by a swelling at the base of the flower) with a fine paintbrush.

Harvest: Check your plants daily once fruit appears, as cucumbers ripen at breakneck speed. Cut them from the stem with a knife, at the size indicated for the variety, usually 15 to 20 cm (6 to 8 in.) long for slicing, or 5 to 10 cm (2 to 4 in.) for pickling. Harvesting encourages more production; overripe cucumbers inhibit fruit set. Refrigerate cucumbers after harvest.

Save Seeds: Allow the fruit to ripen on the vine past the edible stage, until it's golden yellow. Scoop the pulp and seeds into a non-metallic container and ferment as described in Chapter 3 or dry them on a screen.

Serve: Slice fresh cucumbers into salads and sandwiches, or grate them and mix with yogurt and seasonings such as dill or lemon and garlic to make refreshing dips. Any bitter taste can be removed by peeling, as the compounds that cause it accumulate in the skin.

Preserve: Many cultivars can be preserved as pickles.

Suggested Cultivars
Gynoecious cucumbers (female flowers)
'Calypso' is a productive, disease-resis-tant hybrid that is good for pickles and slicing.
'Ultra Pak' is an early, hybrid slicing type, produced on a semi-bush plant that grows well in a container.

Monoecious cucumbers (male and female flowers)
'Fanfare' is a disease-resistant, semi-bush hybrid slicing type that is suitable for a container.
'Lemon' is an heirloom vine from the 1890s that produces round, yellow fruit that is good in salads. This novelty cucumber is rarely found in markets.
'Marketmore 76' is a productive, disease-resistant, open-pollinated slicing type, developed at Cornell University.
'Morden Early' is an early hybrid developed by the Morden Research Centre in Morden, Manitoba. It produces 10 cm (4 in.) fruit, suitable for fresh use or pickling.
'Northern Pickling' is a popular, early, open-pollinated pickling type, produced on a semi-bush plant that is suitable for a container.
'Salad Bush' is a compact hybrid plant that was developed to be grown in containers.
'Straight 8' is a productive, late-maturing American heirloom from 1935 that yields slicers.
'Sweet Slice' is an early, disease-resistant hybrid slicer, bred for thin skin and mild flavour.

Eggplant ... *For the Enthusiastic Gardener*

Solanum melongena

Family: nightshade (*Solanaceae*)

Type: warm-season perennial grown as an annual

Height: 45 cm (18 in.) or taller

Space: 45 cm (18 in.)

Light: full sun

Propagation: seed indoors in mid-March, transplant outdoors in early June

Seed Viability: retains 50% germination for 7 years

Eggplants originate from tropical Asia and were first cultivated in India. A long growing season with plenty of heat is necessary to produce these gorgeous, glossy oval fruits.

'Dusky' eggplant

How to grow: Eggplants must be set outdoors as transplants, and benefit from the soil warmth generated by plastic mulch. Seed indoors 0.5 cm (0.25 in.) deep, and transplant seedlings with one pair of true leaves into individual containers. If the root-ball fills the container, move the seedlings into a larger pot.

Set transplants outdoors when the soil temperature is at least 15°C (60°F), and surround them with a collar to foil cutworms. Transplant through plastic mulch and install supported crop covers over them to retain warmth. Some cultivars require support with a tomato cage. Eggplant can be grown in a container in a hot location.

Remove the crop cover when temperatures warm and blossoms form. The temperature must be above 21°C (70°F) to set fruit. Flea beetles will damage this plant; floating row covers are useful to control them.

Harvest: Harvest when the fruits are the size indicated for the cultivar, and the skin is glossy and the flesh feels springy. Cut the eggplant from the plant with a sharp knife, leaving a short stem attached. Refrigerate eggplant after harvest.

Serve: Eggplant must be cooked before it is consumed. To prevent it from getting greasy during cooking, peel the thick skin off, unless it is young and tender, and then slice or cube the fruit. Sprinkle the pieces with salt and leave them in a colander for one hour. Rinse and pat the pieces dry, and then grill, roast, or fry them according to your recipe. Eggplant is an ingredient of *ratatouille*, a French vegetable stew. It is also delicious roasted and puréed with olive oil, lemon juice, and garlic in the Middle Eastern dip, *baba ghanoush*.

Suggested Cultivars

'Black Beauty' is an heirloom that produces large, dark purple fruit.

'Dusky' is a hybrid that is productive in a wide range of weather conditions.

'Fairytale' is an early hybrid that produces 10 cm (4 in.), seedless, lavender-and-white-striped fruit on an attractive, compact plant that is suitable for containers.

Marjoram, Sweet

Origanum majorana
Family: mint (*Lamiaceae*)
Type: tender warm-season perennial, usually grown as annual.
Height: 30 cm (12 in.)
Space: 20 cm (8 in.)

Sweet marjoram

Light: full sun
Propagation: seed indoors in mid-March, transplant outdoors after frost date
Seed Viability: 2 years

Native to northern Africa and southwest Asia, sweet marjoram looks very similar to its close cousin, oregano. It forms a compact plant with small, slightly hairy leaves arranged along upright, purplish stems. An alternate common name, "knotted marjoram," refers to its flower buds, which resemble round knots on slender spikes above the leaves. The buds open into inconspicuous, tiny white or pale pink blossoms.

How to grow: Seed indoors eight weeks before the spring frost date. Press the tiny seeds into the soil surface, but don't completely cover them as light promotes germination. Set transplants outdoors after the danger of frost has passed.

Place marjoram against a south-facing wall where it can soak up extra warmth. It makes an attractive ground cover or an excellent container plant, mixed with other herbs. Full sun and good drainage are necessary to maintain a robust plant.

Harvest: Fragrant, spicy leaves can be cut throughout the summer; the essential oils are strongest just before the flower buds open. This is a good stage to harvest the plant for drying, by cutting the stems back to the ground.

Save Seeds: Allow some flowers to bloom; as the seed-stalks dry, shake them into a paper sack.

Serve: Sweet marjoram can be substituted for oregano in recipes, and it especially complements beans.

Preserve: Preserve sweet marjoram by drying leafy stems.

Melons ... *For the Enthusiastic Gardener*

Cucumis melo
Family: gourd (*Cucurbitaceae*)
Type: warm-season annual
Height: vine
Space: 1 to 1.2 m (3 to 4 ft.)
Light: full sun
Propagation: seed outdoors under cover in late May; seed indoors in early May, transplant outdoors in late May to early June
Seed Viability: 5 years

Melons were domesticated from wild plants in tropical and subtropical Africa. True to their African roots, these plants require at least three months of hot weather to produce sweet, succulent fruit.

How to Grow: Choose melon cultivars that mature in seventy-five to eighty-five days from transplant. Muskmelon (typically called cantaloupe in North America) is the most likely to succeed in prairie gardens, but it's also possible to grow honeydew, crenshaw, and ca-nary melon. Warm the soil with plastic mulch before planting.

Melons grown from transplants produce earlier and yield more than direct seeded plants. Seed them indoors, 1 cm (0.5 in.) deep with the pointed end of the seed facing up, in individual pots that are 7.5 cm (3 in.) deep, three weeks before you plan to set them outdoors. Transplant seedlings with one or two true leaves outdoors, when the danger of frost has passed, through slits in the plastic mulch, and install a supported crop cover. Handle the taproot carefully during transplanting.

Melons can be seeded outdoors, near the frost date if the soil has been pre-warmed to at least 15°C (60°F). Aim to produce one melon plant per square metre (sq. yd.); sow twice the number of seeds for the space you have and thin to the strongest seedlings. Plant through holes cut into plastic mulch, and cover the planted area with a clear plastic cold frame to trap heat and accelerate growth.

If frost is in the forecast, cover the cold frame with a blanket before

'Athena' muskmelon

'Earli-Dew' honeydew   'Burpee Early Hybrid' crenshaw melon   'Dorado' canary melons

sundown. Melons prefer temperatures above 13°C (55°F) and an insulating blanket is warranted when night temperatures drop below 10°C (50°F) any time during the season. Clear plastic cold frames must be ventilated on sunny days if outdoor air temperatures rise above 21°C (70°F). Remove crop covers when they restrict vine growth.

Melons produce separate male and female flowers on the same plant. Male flowers appear first; female flowers look like a tiny melon with yellow petals. Bees pollinate the flowers, but their access is limited when plants are covered. To increase fruit set, transfer pollen with a fine paintbrush from male flowers to female flowers during mid to late morning.

Keep the soil evenly moist until the fruit reaches mature size, and reduce irrigation during ripening to prevent cracking.

Harvest: Ripening cues vary among melon cultivars. Muskmelons develop prominent netting over their skin, emit a sweet, earthy fragrance at the stem end, and separate easily from the vine (a stage that is called "full slip"). Canary and crenshaw melons change colour when ripe; they don't slip from the vine. Honeydew may develop a light netting on its pale green skin as it matures, or feel slightly soft. The best way to determine if a melon is ripe is to cut it open and taste it! When frost threatens at the end of the season, bring full-size melons indoors. At room temperature, the fruit will continue ripening.

Ripe melons should be stored at room temperature, where they remain at peak quality for only a few days, except canary melons, which keep well up to two months.

Save Seeds: Melons are insect-pollinated and all cultivars can cross with each other; melons in this group don't cross with watermelons, which are a different species. Seeds of all melons, including watermelons, are ripe when the melon is ready to eat. Separate the seeds from the flesh; add water, discard the hollow seeds that float, and dry the solid viable seeds.

Serve: The best way to enjoy home-grown melon is sliced fresh from the vine.

Suggested Cultivars

Canary Melon

'Dorado' is a hybrid, disease-resistant canary melon with bright yellow skin, white flesh and tough rind that stores well.

Crenshaw Melon

'Burpee Early Hybrid' is a large, early, hybrid crenshaw melon with yellow-green skin and salmon flesh.

'Vista' watermelon

Honeydew

'Earli-Dew' is a disease-resistant, early, hybrid, smooth-skinned, lime green honeydew.

Muskmelon

'Athena' is a popular hybrid muskmelon that rivals large market fruit.

'Fastbreak' is one of the earliest hybrid muskmelons.

'Nutmeg' is an early, open-pollinated muskmelon with golden-green flesh.

Related Species ... For the Enthusiastic Gardener

Watermelon (*Citrullus lanatus*) is a warm-season annual, cultivated like other melons, but it requires more heat and space to produce. Set three-week-old watermelon transplants outdoors in early June after warming the soil. Use black plastic mulch and floating row covers for extra warmth, and space the plants 1.2 to 2 m (4 to 6.5 ft.) apart. When ripe, the fruit changes colour on the "ground-spot," where it rests on the ground, to white or golden yellow. Watermelon keeps up to two weeks at room temperature, although it continues to ripen and quality deteriorates after just a few days.

Suggested Cultivars

'Black Tail Mountain' is an early open-pollinated cultivar that produces round fruit.

'Crimson Sweet' is an open-pollinated heirloom that produces large, classic fruit.

'Early Moonbeam' is an open-pollinated cultivar with yellow flesh.

'Jade Star' is an improved hybrid of 'Sugar Baby' that produces uniform, small, round fruit.

'New Queen' is a productive hybrid that produces small fruit with orange flesh.

'Sugar Baby' is open-pollinated, early, and produces small fruit.

'Vista' is an early hybrid that produces large, classic fruit.

Peppers ... *For the Enthusiastic Gardener*

Capsicum annuum
Family: nightshade (*Solanaceae*)
Type: warm-season annual
Height: up to 75 cm (30 in.)
Space: 30 to 45 cm (12 to 18 in.)
Light: full sun
Propagation: seed indoors in mid to late March, transplant outdoors in early June
Seed Viability: retains 50% germination for 3 years

Peppers were domesticated in Mexico, Central and South America thousands of years before Europeans came to the New World. Hungarians quickly adopted the plant after it was brought to Europe in the fifteenth century, and set to selecting short-season peppers for their cool climate. As a result, many early-maturing, open-pollinated cultivars hail from Hungary.

Sweet peppers and chile peppers are the same species; green bell peppers are unripe sweet peppers. All peppers produce chemicals called capsaicinoids that create spicy flavour, but hot peppers contain larger amounts. During ripening, the "heat-producing" chemicals accumulate in the soft tissue surrounding the seeds, and hot growing conditions intensify the fiery flavour. These chemicals help ward off rodents that eat the fruit in the wild and soil fungi that might cause disease and interfere with germination.

How to Grow: Peppers must be set outdoors as transplants. Choose cultivars that mature in less than seventy-five days from transplant. The number of days to maturity usually refers to how long the cultivar takes to produce green peppers; it takes longer for the fruit to change colour. Before transplanting, warm the soil with plastic mulch.

Seed indoors, 0.5 cm (0.25 in) deep, eight weeks before the frost date, and mist the sprouting seedlings to help the seed coat pop off. Transplant young seedlings to a pot that is 10 cm (4 in.) deep.

Transplant peppers outdoors, one to two weeks after the last frost, when the soil temperature is at least 15°C (60°F). Protect them from cutworms with a collar. Supported floating row covers and plastic mulch are recommended to increase warmth and provide shelter from wind. An alternative is to wrap clear plastic around a tomato cage, leaving the top open until the plants start blooming. Peppers can also be grown in containers in a warm location.

Remove row covers as flowering begins. Peppers are self-pollinated and cross-pollinated by insects. You can aid pollination by agitating the flowers every morning. Pepper plants need consistently moist soil to avoid problems with blossom end rot, where the fruit becomes sunken, dark, or dry at the base.

Harvest: Peppers can be harvested at any stage, but their flavour develops with maturity. After the fruit reaches mature size, it changes colour from green to yellow, orange, red, or purple. Ripening is usually cut short on the prairies, so peppers are often harvested green. Harvest by cutting the fruit off the plant, leaving a stem attached. Use gloves when handling hot peppers.

Once the outdoor temperature remains below 12°C (54°F) during the day for more than a week in autumn, harvest the fruit and bring it indoors. Lay full-size peppers in a single layer on cardboard boxes and allow them to continue ripening at room temperature. Treat small fruit as green peppers, refrigerate them, and use them promptly. Refrigerate ripe peppers after harvest.

Save Seeds: Save seeds only from unblemished fruit that has completely changed colour on the vine.

'Mariachi' peppers

Serve: Green peppers are excellent stuffed and baked. Sauté peppers with fresh onions, tomatoes, and garlic to make a delicious Hungarian dish called *lecsó* that is served with bread or pasta.

The best way to cool the heat from eating spicy peppers is to drink or eat a dairy product.

Preserve: Peppers can be frozen without blanching them first. Remove the seeds and stem, and then chop them. Spread chopped peppers on a tray and freeze them for one hour. Place the chopped pieces in an airtight container in the freezer, and remove them as needed for recipes.

Suggested Cultivars

'Fat 'N Sassy' is an early, hybrid bell-shaped sweet pepper.

'Feherozon' is an early, open-pollinated Hungarian variety with semi-sweet, pale yellow, tapered fruit that matures to orange; this cultivar tolerates cool weather.

'Gypsy' is an early, hybrid tapered pepper.

'Hungarian Yellow Wax Hot' is a productive, Hungarian heirloom with spicy, long, tapered fruit that tolerates cool weather.

'Mariachi' is an early hybrid that forms a compact plant with mildly pungent, tapered peppers.

'Mucho Nacho' is an early, hybrid jalapeno-type with spicy fruit.

'Pepperoncini' is open-pollinated and produces slender, wrinkled fruit.

'Sweet Banana' (also called 'Hungarian Wax Sweet') is a Hungarian heirloom with long, tapered fruit.

Perilla

Perilla frutescens
Family: mint (*Lamiaceae*)
Type: warm-season annual
Height: 30 to 45 cm (12 to 18 in.) or taller
Space: 25 cm (10 in.)
Light: full sun to part shade
Propagation: seed indoors in mid-March, transplant outdoors after frost date; seed outdoors after the frost date
Seed Viability: 1 year at room temperature, 5 years if frozen

Native to the Himalayas, perilla is widely grown and used in Asia, and it is known as *shiso* in Japan. In its natural habitat, the oily seeds are a food source for birds. Perilla's sweet and spicy foliage is similar to basil, but not as potent. The plant has deeply toothed, heart-shaped leaves that are clothed with tiny hairs.

How to Grow: Seed perilla outdoors after the spring frost date, when the soil warms in late May or early June, or seed indoors at room temperature six weeks before the frost date and transplant seedlings outdoors when all danger of frost has passed. To accelerate sprouting, soak the seeds for one to two hours prior to sowing them.

Perilla

Barely cover the seeds with soil as light promotes germination.

Perilla looks attractive in a container if it is kept pinched back to retain a bushy form. It is sensitive to day-length and long nights trigger purple or white flowers to form. In the garden, perilla self-seeds readily.

Harvest: Pick leafy stems just before using them, and store the stalks in a glass of water at room temperature. Harvest seeds for seasoning by tapping dry seed stalks into a paper envelope.

Save Seeds: Collect seeds for planting in the same manner as for seasoning. Dry the seeds in the envelope for two weeks after harvesting and store them in an airtight container in the freezer to retain viability.

Serve: Perilla makes a beautiful garnish or herbal vinegar, and is valued as a pickling herb in Japanese cuisine. Slivered into a fresh cucumber salad with a dressing made of equal parts vinegar and sugar, perilla's flavour is reminiscent of basil and mint. The leaves can also be marinated in equal proportions vinegar and sugar and rolled around sushi as a substitute for *nori*. The flower buds add flavour when sprinkled on salads and the seeds can be tossed with steamed rice.

Suggested Cultivar

'Atropurpurea' is a handsome cultivar with deep purple leaves.

The narrow foliage of summer savory (on the right) is very aromatic.

Savory, Summer
Satureja hortensis
Family: mint (*Lamiaceae*)
Type: warm-season annual
Height: 30 cm (12 in.)
Space: 20 cm (8 in.)
Light: full sun
Propagation: seed indoors in late March, transplant outdoors after the frost date; seed outdoors after the frost date
Seed Viability: 1 year

Hailing from the Mediterranean, spicy summer savory is often called the "bean herb" because the two flavours pair so well. A perennial species, winter savory (*Satureja montana*) is also cultivated, but it is used less often as summer savory is sweeter.

How to Grow: Seed indoors, six weeks before the frost date. Press the tiny seeds into the soil, but do not completely cover them because light promotes germination. Transplant the seedlings outdoors after the danger of frost has passed. Summer savory can also be sown directly outdoors after the last frost.

Summer savory relishes hot, dry spots, and grows very quickly. Pinch the stems back on young seedlings to encourage robust growth, and to form a bushy plant.

Harvest: Clip sprigs of small, narrow leaves for fresh use when the plants reach 15 cm (6 in.). When the tiny white flowers appear, harvest the plant for drying.

Save Seeds: Allow plants to flower, and collect the stalks into a paper bag as the lower fruits dry. After they are completely dry, rub them on a screen to separate seeds.

Serve: Mince fresh summer savory leaves into soft butter and add a dab to steamed vegetables; its peppery zest goes particularly well with green beans.

Preserve: Preserve summer savory by hanging the stems to dry. Strip the dry leaves off the stems before storing them.

Squash, Summer
Cucurbita pepo
Family: gourd (*Cucurbitaceae*)
Type: warm-season annual

Height: bush types 90 cm (36 in.), or vine
Space: minimum 90 cm (36 in.), depending on the cultivar
Light: full sun
Propagation: seed outdoors in late May to early June; seed indoors in early May, transplant outdoors after the frost date
Seed Viability: 4 years

Native to balmy regions of Mexico and Central America, ancient squash plants

'Gold Rush' zucchini

bore small, hard fruit and were origi-nally cultivated for their nutritious, ed-ible seeds. As squash was domesticated, selection for larger seeds also increased the fleshy portion of the fruit and made it a desirable diet staple. Modern cultivars come in a dazzling assortment of shapes, sizes, and colours, with culi-nary possibilities from the flower bud stage to mature fruit.

Botanists divide garden squashes into three species, but gardeners divide this vegetable into summer and winter squash, determined by when the fruit is harvested and used. Summer squash is consumed immature, when it is small, tender and thin-skinned. In contrast, winter squash is vine-ripened until it develops a hard rind that pre-serves the fruit so it can be stored into winter. Summer squash, like zucchini, is more popular than winter squash because it produces early and abun-dantly on large, but relatively compact plants. Winter squash is described below for the enthusiastic gardener with more space.

How to Grow: Studies show that squash grown from transplants produces earlier and yields more than direct seeded plants, but the advantage of direct seeding is the unrestricted ability of the plant to produce a taproot.

Seed outdoors, 2.5 cm (1 in.) deep with the pointed end of the seed facing up, after the frost date, when the soil temperature warms to at least 15°C (60°F).

Seed indoors, in individual pots that are 7.5 cm (3 in.) deep, three weeks before you plan to set them outdoors. Set transplants with one or two true leaves outdoors after the dan-ger of frost has passed, usually in late May to early June. For extra warmth and wind protection, use a supported floating row cover until it restricts vine growth and blossoms appear. Avoid wetting the plant leaves when irrigat-ing to prevent mildew.

Separate male and female flowers are produced on the same plant and pollinated by bees. The first blossoms are usually male. The female flower has a swelling at its base that resembles a tiny squash. Use males to prepare ed-ible flowers, leaving a few to pollinate the females, and allow the female flow-ers to produce fruit.

Harvest: Once the vines start produc-ing, check them daily and harvest often to encourage new fruit pro-duction. Summer squash should be harvested young and tender, when it is less than 5 cm (2 in.) in diameter and 7.5 to 15 cm (3 to 6 in.) long, or the size indicated for the cultivar. Cut the fruit from the plant with a knife, leav-ing a 2.5 cm (1 in.) stem attached.

Harvest blossoms for frying just as the petals open in the morning. Rinse them and refrigerate them in ice water for use the same day.

Save Seeds: Different cultivars of the same squash species can cross with each other, and must be separated by 0.8 km (0.5 mi.) to keep pure seeds. Isolate your designated seed-saving plants with floating row covers and hand-pollinate them according to the instructions in Chapter 3. Be aware that there is a lot of confusion among squash names, and that pumpkins, spaghetti squash, and acorn squash belong to the same species as summer squash.

Leave summer squash on the vine past the ripe stage until the skin becomes tough, as the seeds need at least six weeks to mature. Save plump seeds only; rinse them and dry them on screens until they become brittle.

Serve: Add summer squash to salads or stir-fries. Salvage over-ripe zucchini by grating it, and baking it into muffins or bread. Squash blossoms are a delicacy, stuffed with ricotta cheese and fresh chopped herbs, then dipped in batter or breadcrumbs and lightly fried until tender.

Preserve: Zucchini freezes well, if the excess moisture is removed first. Shred it, salt it, and drain it over a colander, pressing out as much water as possible before freezing it.

Suggested Cultivars

'Costata Romanesco' is an Italian heirloom that bears long, slender, medium green fruit with light green ribs.

'Early Yellow Summer Crookneck' is a warty, yellow crookneck heirloom from 1700.

'Eight Ball' is a productive hybrid with small, round, dark green fruit.

'Gold Rush' is a hybrid zucchini that produces straight yellow fruit with a dark green stem.

'Italian Largo' is a hybrid that produces green striped fruit that is very similar to 'Costata Romanesco.'

'Multipik' is a productive hybrid that produces yellow straightneck fruit.

'Peter Pan' is a hybrid patty-pan squash that produces small, light green scalloped fruit on a compact bush plant.

'Spineless Beauty' is an early, hybrid green zucchini with no spines on the stems or leaves, so it is easy to pick.

'Starship' is a very early, hybrid patty-pan squash with small, dark green fruit.

'Sunburst' is a hybrid patty-pan squash

Mature 'Buttercup' winter squashes

'Ambercup' winter squashes

Female 'Buttercup' squash blossoms have a miniature swelling at the base that resembles the squash.

A male 'Buttercup' squash blossom

that produces small, bright yellow scalloped fruit.

'Sundance' is a hybrid yellow crookneck with smooth skin.

Related Species ... For the Enthusiastic Gardener
Winter Squash

Three species of winter squash are grown in prairie gardens (*Curcurbita maxima*, *Curcurbita moschata*, and *Curcurbita pepo*); to make matters confusing, pumpkins, spaghetti squash, and acorn squash belong to the same species as summer squash, but they are harvested mature like winter squash.

Winter squash is cultivated similar to summer squash, but the extensive vines must be spaced at least 1.8 to 2.4 m (6 to 8 ft.) apart, and it takes more time to produce mature fruit. A few new hybrids produce on bush plants. Choose cultivars that mature in less than one hundred days. Those with a maturity date of less than eighty-five days can be seeded outdoors, but most cultivars should be sown indoors three weeks ahead of transplanting them in the garden. Warm the soil with plastic before planting.

Seed indoors, 2.5 cm (1 in.) deep, in individual pots that are 7.5 cm (3 in.) deep, in early May. Transplant seedlings with one or two true leaves outdoors, after the danger of frost has passed in late May to early June. Take care not to disturb the root during transplanting.

For extra warmth, sow seeds or set transplants out through slits in plastic mulch, and install a supported floating row cover until it restricts vine growth. The plastic mulch can be left in place all season. Avoid wetting plant leaves during irrigation to prevent mildew.

Harvest: Winter squash is mature when the fruit reaches full size, attains deep colour and the rind is too hard to be pierced with a fingernail.

Harvest before frost to prevent slight tissue damage that can become an entry for rot. Green fruits will continue to ripen and change colour in storage, but the flavour may be inferior to vine-ripened fruit.

Pumpkins for carving can be left on the vine until temperatures are forecast to dip below -1°C (30°F). Your pumpkins will have a better chance of ripening if you limit the number produced; simply remove the blossoms after a few form. Once harvested, pumpkins will continue to develop orange colour at room temperature.

Cut the fruit from the vine, leaving a 5 cm (2 in.) stem attached, but don't carry it by the stem. Cure squash by storing it for two weeks indoors in a warm room. After curing, store squash in a single layer, in a cool, dry place, and check frequently for soft spots or mould. Winter squash keeps several weeks to several months at 10°C (50°F), depending on the level of maturity it reached and the variety. Don't refrigerate winter squash, or it will deteriorate.

Seeds of winter squash can be saved from mature fruit, in the same manner as summer squash. Different cultivars of the same species can cross with each other.

Serve: The simplest way to prepare winter squash is to cut it in half, scoop out the seeds, place it cut side down in a pan with 2.5 cm (1 in.) of water, and bake it at 180°C (350°F) for one hour or until tender. To sweeten, turn the halves over and place 15 ml (1 Tbsp.) of brown sugar and 5 ml (1 tsp.) of butter in the cavity and bake ten minutes more. Scoop baked squash out of the shell and serve it as a table vegetable or purée it and make it into muffins, soup, or pumpkin-style pie.

Preserve: Cooked squash flesh can be frozen.

Suggested Cultivars (listed by species)
Curcurbita maxima

'Ambercup' is a hybrid buttercup type with a bright orange exterior, and dry sweet flesh.

'Autumn Cup' is a hybrid, dark green buttercup type with small, dark green fruit, produced on a compact bush plant.

'Buttercup' is an open-pollinated, classic buttercup type with small, dark green fruit and rich, moist, sweet orange flesh.

'Gold Nugget' is an open-pollinated, productive, compact bush plant that produces small, round orange fruit.

Curcurbita moschata

'Early Butternut' is an early hybrid butternut type that produces high quality fruit.

Curcurbita pepo

'Baby Bear' is a very small, hybrid pie pumpkin with semi-hull-less seeds that are good for roasting.

'Bush Spirit' (also known as 'Spirit Hybrid') is a hybrid small pumpkin produced on a relatively compact plant.

'Small Sugar' (also known as 'New England Pie') is an heirloom pie pumpkin from 1863 that produces small fruit.

'Rouge Vif D'Etampes' is a French heirloom that produces large, reddish, flat pumpkins that are good for pies.

'Sugar Loaf' is an open-pollinated, improved 'Delicata' type, also known as sweet potato squash. Its long vines bear striking cream and green-striped fruit with sweet yellow-orange flesh.

'Table Ace' is an early, productive, hybrid acorn type with dark green fruit on a compact, semi-bush plant.

'Vegetable Spaghetti' is an open-pollinated, hard-shelled summer squash, with pale, creamy green skin. It is baked or steamed and consumed like spaghetti pasta.

Sweet Potato ... *For the Enthusiastic Gardener*

Ipomea batatas
Family: morning glory (*Convovulaceae*)
Type: warm-season perennial, grown as annual
Height: vine
Space: 30 to 45 cm (12 to 18 in.)
Light: full sun
Propagation: Plant slips outdoors

after the frost date in late May to early June

Sweet potatoes are widely cultivated in the tropics and are thought to have originated from a wild plant in tropical South America. The sweet, moist, orange-fleshed edible tuberous roots are produced on a pretty, trailing vine. Sweet potatoes are often confused with yams, another tropical species with a dry, pale, swollen root. Amazingly, one short-season cultivar has been developed for regions with one hundred frost-free days; it will produce in any garden that can ripen tomatoes if you warm the soil and use crop covers.

How to Grow: Sweet potatoes are usually grown from a 20 to 30 cm (8 to 12 in.) vine section, called a slip. Slips are produced by suppliers of sweet potato stock, and shipped at planting time. Supermarket tubers aren't short-season cultivars. To propagate your own slips from seed tubers harvested the previous season, bring them into a warm place (24°C [75°F]) eight to ten weeks before the frost date. Immerse the bottom half in a jar of warm water. Within a couple weeks it should sprout, and it takes about six weeks for the sprouts to grow 20 cm (8 in.). Cut the sprouts from the tuber and root them in water for a few days, or transplant bare-root plants directly outdoors.

Before planting, warm the soil with plastic mulch. Acclimate slips slowly to outdoor light and transplant them

'Georgia Jet' sweet potato vine and blossom
PHOTO - KEN ALLAN

'Georgia Jet' sweet potatoes
PHOTO - KEN ALLAN

after the danger of frost has passed, when the soil is at least 18°C (65°F). Slit the plastic and insert the slip, planting it horizontally, such that 15 cm (6 in.) of the stem is buried 7.5 cm (3 in.) deep. The slip roots where it is covered by soil, and tubers expand from roots. If the slip is planted vertically, it will produce fewer, but larger tubers. Seal the cut edges of the plastic with soil, so it remains taut around the base of the plant.

Sweet potatoes can be grown in large containers in a hot location. Use a potting mix that contains two parts soil and one part compost, and plant one slip per container.

Install a clear plastic supported crop cover over the plants to create a warm, humid environment, protected from wind. Do not allow the leaves to touch the plastic, and cover the frame with a blanket if night temperatures are forecast to drop below 10°C (50°F).

Keep the soil evenly moist, irrigating with warm water if possible. Remove the crop cover as it restricts vine growth. Monitor temperatures and cover the plants with floating row covers on nights that are forecast to go below 10°C (50°F). Leave the plastic mulch in place all season.

Harvest: Immediately after the first frost, lift the tubers with a digging fork. Handle them carefully to avoid bruising and wash the soil off. Sweet potatoes don't tolerate soil temperatures below 12°C (55°F) for more than a few days and must be dug within one week after the first frost. Potted plants need to be harvested earlier than those grown in the ground, because the soil cools faster in containers.

Cure sweet potatoes immediately after harvest by storing them in a very warm place, in paper bags or perforated plastic bags to maintain humidity. At 30°C (85°F), curing takes one week. At 27°C (80°F) it takes two weeks to cure, and sprouting might be initiated. Curing at warm temperatures greatly enhances sweetness and makes the skin impermeable to moisture.

Cured sweet potatoes will keep about six months at room temperature, or eight months at 15°C (60°F). Rub off any sprouts that appear; if this is done quickly the tuber will be unaffected. Don't refrigerate sweet potatoes as refrigeration causes chilling injury.

Save Seed: Save small 2.5 cm (1 in.) tubers from your best plants as planting stock for next year. Cure them and store them in a cool, dry place in paper bags.

Serve: Bake sweet potatoes at 180°C (350°F) for one to two hours until tender, and scoop the flesh out of the skin before serving.

Preserve: Baked sweet potato flesh can be frozen.

Suggested Cultivar

'Georgia Jet' is an early-maturing, high-yielding cultivar for cool, short seasons that stores well. It can be grown in areas with 90 to 100 frost-free days.

Tomato

Lycopersicon esculentum
Family: nightshade (*Solanaceae*)
Type: warm-season annual
Height: determinate bush up to 90 cm (36 in.), or indeterminate vine 1.5 m (5 ft.)
Space: 45 to 60 cm (18 to 24 in.) or more, depending on the cultivar
Light: full sun
Propagation: seed indoors in late March, transplant outdoors after frost date
Seed Viability: 4 years or more, depending on cultivar

It's believed that tomatoes were domesticated in Mexico from tiny-fruited plants that were native to Central and South America. Attaining vine-ripened fruit is the pinnacle of home gardens today, but the tomato was regarded with suspicion when Spanish explorers brought it to Europe in the early 1500s because it is related to other poisonous plants.

A tomato cage is sufficient to support determinate tomato plants such as 'Taxi'.

'Sunsugar' cherry tomatoes

'Early Girl' tomatoes

Use sturdy stakes to support
indeterminate vine tomatoes.

Tomatoes are produced on two types of plants: long, indeterminate vines and short, determinate bushes, and the potential to grow tall or short is pre-determined by the genetic background of the cultivar, no matter how well you take care of it.

Determinate bush cultivars are programmed to stop growing at a certain size and to produce a flower cluster at the end of each branch. All tomatoes on the same plant ripen within a relatively short period of time, which is desirable when you want to make sauce, can, dehydrate or freeze them. The compact form of determinate plants is suitable for containers.

Indeterminate vine varieties produce a series of leaves and a flower cluster in a continuous progression until frost. The plant requires staking and should be limited to one or two main vines. Trained upright, vines take up less space than bush tomatoes, and once production begins, vines bear tomatoes that ripen in sequence until the end of the season.

The oblong paste or plum tomato has solid flesh with little water and is great for making sauce, freezing, canning, or drying. All other tomatoes, from petite 2.5 cm (1 in.) cherry globes to huge 15 cm (6 in.) beefsteak slicers are best savoured fresh from the vine.

How to Grow: Tomatoes must be set outdoors as transplants, and the days to maturity for each cultivar are based on setting out transplants. Early cultivars are more likely to produce mature fruit without extra effort to extend the season. Warm the soil and use crop covers to extend the season for later maturing cultivars.

Seed indoors, 0.5 cm (0.25 in.) deep, six to eight weeks before the frost date. Tomato seedlings grow so rapidly that it's best not to sow earlier, unless you are prepared to grow individual seedlings in fairly large pots.

Tomato plants tolerate minimum soil temperatures of 10°C (50°F) and can be set out near the frost date if they are insulated with water-filled plastic cones specifically designed for this purpose. Otherwise, set transplants outdoors after the danger of frost has passed, usually late May to early June. Place collars around the seedlings to prevent cutworm damage. Install a tomato cage around determinate types. Tie indeterminate tomatoes to 1.8 m (6 ft.) stakes, buried 30 cm (1 ft.) in the ground, with strips of flexible material, like old stockings.

Pinch off any side shoots that sprout on indeterminate vines to direct the plant's energy into producing ripe tomatoes on the main vine. Do not prune determinate plants because there are a finite number of fruit-producing stems.

Most tomato roots are in the top 30 cm (1 ft.) of soil, and studies have shown that they don't compete well with other crops planted between them. Young plants benefit from warmth and wind protection offered by supported crop covers early in the season. Tomatoes are mostly self-pollinated by agitation from wind. If night temperatures fall below 12°C (55°F), the flowers drop off.

Tomatoes grow rapidly in size, but the ripening process is much slower. As the fruit matures, it becomes pale green, softens, and the final colour gradually evolves. Flavour progressively develops as long as the tomato remains on the vine and the weather is warm.

The most common problem is blossom end rot, where the bottom of the tomato becomes dark, sunken, and tough. It is usually caused by uneven soil moisture, especially if the soil dries during sudden hot weather, and can be prevented by irrigating deeply and applying mulch.

Harvest: Pick tomatoes when they become the appropriate colour for the cultivar and separate easily from the vine. At season's end, when daytime temperatures fall below 12°C (54°F) for a week, harvest any green tomatoes that have reached full size and bring them indoors. Store them one-layer deep in a cardboard box, at room temperature. Tomatoes that matured sufficiently on the plant will eventually change colour indoors, but won't have the same rich taste of vine-ripened ones. Store tomatoes at room temperature; refrigeration causes them to become bland.

Save Seeds: Allow tomatoes to ripen completely on the vine, and separate the seeds from the pulp. Follow the instructions for fermenting them in Chapter 3, or dry them on a screen.

Serve: Slice fresh tomatoes in sandwiches or salad. To make a fast, fresh tomato topping for a single serving of spaghetti squash, pasta, *bruschetta*, or pizza: chop one juicy, vine-ripened tomato with two fresh basil leaves, and drizzle the mix with less than 1 ml (1/4 tsp) of olive oil. Microwave for one minute or less, and enjoy with fresh grated Parmesan cheese.

Preserve: Freeze whole paste tomatoes or dry 0.5 cm (0.25 in.) thick slices in a food dehydrator.

Suggested Cultivars
Bush (determinate)
'Black Plum' is an open-pollinated paste tomato with a purplish shoulder.

'Mamma Mia' is a heavy-yielding hybrid paste tomato.

'Manitoba' is an early, open-pollinated Canadian cultivar from the Morden Research Centre.

'Patio' is a compact hybrid that makes an ideal container plant.

'Starfire' is an open-pollinated cultivar with large, red fruit, developed specifically for the Canadian prairies at the Morden Research Centre.

'Silvery Fir Tree' is an early Russian heirloom that forms a compact plant with attractive dissected foliage, suitable for containers.

'Sub-Arctic Maxi' is an early compact Canadian hybrid that is suitable for a container, developed for the Alberta climate at the Beaverlodge Research Station.

'Taxi' is a mid-season, open-pollinated heirloom with bright yellow fruit.

'Tumbler' is a hybrid cherry tomato that is ideal for hanging baskets.

Vine (indeterminate)
'Big Beef' is a popular large-fruited, mid-season hybrid.

'Celebrity' is a disease-resistant hybrid with good-sized fruit.

'Early Girl' is an early hybrid with small fruit on a compact plant.

'Lemon Boy' is a disease-resistant, late-season hybrid with yellow fruit.

'Long Keeper' is an open-pollinated, late-season, orange-red tomato that has thick skin and an incredibly long shelf life.

'Oxheart' is an heirloom late-season cultivar with large, heart-shaped red fruit.

'Red Currant' is an heirloom that produces tiny red tomatoes on rambling vines. 'Yellow Currant' is similar with yellow fruit.

'Stupice' is an early-maturing heirloom from the Czech Republic with small fruit.

'Sun Sugar' is a hybrid that produces sweet, orange cherry tomatoes.

'Sweet Million' is a popular disease-resistant, productive, hybrid cherry tomato.

'Sweet Baby Girl' is a productive, disease-resistant hybrid cherry tomato.

'Yellow Pear' is an heirloom from before 1805 with yellow, pear-shaped 2.5 cm (1 in.) mild-flavoured tomatoes.

Related Species
The Mexican Husk Tomato, or *Tomatillo* (*Physalis ixocarpa*) is a warm-

Tomatillo flowers and fruit

Tomatillo plant

season annual that bears 2.5 to 5 cm (1 to 2 in.) green fruits inside pale green, papery husks. The tomatillo is cultivated like a tomato, and can be grown in a large container such as a barrel. Seed indoors, 0.5 cm (0.25 in.) deep, in early to mid-April, and set transplants outdoors in late May to early June. The plant grows over 90 cm (36 in.) tall, and doesn't require pruning, but a tomato cage is useful to support its sprawling stems. Pick tomatillos when the green fruit almost fills the husk, and the husk splits, and store them in their husks in a paper bag at room temperature. Depending on the stage harvested, tomatillos keep up to a few weeks. To save seeds, allow the fruit to ripen on the plant until it is soft, changes colour (pale yellow

for most varieties), and the husk dries. Separate the seeds from the pulp and dry them on a screen. Tomatillos can self-seed in the garden. To prepare tomatillos, discard the husk and rinse the sticky coating off the fruit. The fruits are usually simmered to soften their skins, before making them into sauces or salsas. Tomatillos, mixed with onion, cilantro, and hot pepper make up a Mexican green salsa known as *salsa verde*. Husked tomatillos can be frozen whole.

Suggested Cultivar
'Toma Verde' is an open-pollinated green tomatillo that makes excellent salsa.

CHAPTER FIVE

Edible Plants for the Permanent Garden: Perennials, Fruiting Shrubs, and Fruit Trees

Asparagus, mint and rhubarb, strawberries and raspberries as well as apple trees and saskatoons are among the permanent edible plants that can define your garden and provide food for your table for years to come.

This chapter is divided into two collections of plant profiles listed by common name in alphabetical order. Perennial plants, including one vegetable and many herbs and small fruits make up the first group. Prairie-hardy woody fruits are covered in the final section.

Each description includes a quick reference to factors that will help you choose plants that suit the conditions of your garden. It indicates how much space or light the plant requires, or whether more than one variety is necessary for cross-pollination. Pay particular attention to the requirements for trees and shrubs, and situate them appropriately as they will become enduring landscape fixtures. Even though perennial plants can be relocated as the garden grows and changes, most of them take three years to become well-rooted and productive, so it's also best to plant them in the right place from the beginning.

Specific cultural advice for each plant regarding propagation, maintenance, or pest control is meant to supplement the general cultivation information provided earlier in the book. Most plants in this chapter will produce well in a range of soils if you follow the recommendations and provide adequate space, light, moisture, and mulch; therefore, soil information is not specified, unless it is deemed necessary. Harvesting, serving, and preserving tips are included for

'Pembina' plums

each crop to help you enjoy your homegrown produce at peak freshness. Some of the best and hardiest new releases and tried-and-true varieties are suggested with the plant descriptions, but the list is by no means comprehensive, and new, improved cultivars are continuously being developed.

Chives, golden oregano, and Italian parsley form a sunny border.

Perennial Vegetable, Herbs, and Small Fruits

Asparagus

Asparagus officinalis
Family: lily (*Liliaceae*)
Type: cool-season perennial
Height: 1 m (3 ft.)
Space: 30 to 45 cm (12 to 18 in.)
Light: full sun to part shade
Propagation: 1- or 2-year-old crowns in early May

It takes at least three summers to establish an asparagus patch, but then it rewards you with the earliest vegetable pickings for years to come. Originally from Europe, asparagus has been grown since ancient Greek times. It escaped from cultivation and has naturalized around the world, so foraging for wild spears is a popular spring activity in many places.

Asparagus spears are actually young stem shoots, which eventually unfold into bright green fronds that resemble a delicate fern. Each plant is either male or female, and while both yield spears, female plants divide their energy between growing sprouts and developing bright red fruits with seeds. As a result, female plants yield fewer spears, and their seedlings can become weedy, so contemporary garden varieties are made up solely of the more productive male plants.

How to Grow: Asparagus is a long-lived crop that requires good drainage and grows best in sandy soil; clay soils need to be loosened with plenty

Asparagus shoot

Asparagus spears unfold into ferny fronds.

of organic matter. To produce a satisfactory harvest, start your patch with at least ten plants, which will eventually fill a bed that is 3 m (10 ft.) long. Asparagus is usually planted from one- or two-year-old crowns of fleshy roots.

Prepare a trench that is 15 cm (6 in.) deep, and place each crown with its roots spread out over a slight mound in the bottom of the trench, and cover the entire crown with 5 cm (2 in.) of soil. As shoots sprout, gradually cover them with soil no deeper than 5 cm (2 in.) at a time, filling the trench by the end of the season.

Apply compost each year after harvesting the spears, or mulch the bed with wood chips, and renew the mulch each year. Keep your asparagus bed free of competing weeds, especially grasses. Irrigate the plants deeply during the growing season and again in late fall after the tops are frosted, but before the soil freezes. Wait until early spring to remove the spent foliage as it helps trap snow that insulates and supplements moisture. If the plants show no signs of pests or disease, chop the leaves and compost them or use them as mulch in the asparagus bed.

Harvest: Asparagus spears emerge in early spring as the soil temperature reaches 10°C (50°F). Refrain from harvesting the first two years after planting. In years three and four, harvest the earliest spears for two weeks only. After the fourth year, asparagus can be harvested each spring for up to six weeks. Snap each 17 cm (7 in.) spear off just above ground level and immerse it briefly in ice water to preserve quality. Stop picking in late June and allow the remaining shoots to open into feathery foliage, which supplies the plant with food reserves for spear production the following spring. Store asparagus in the refrigerator, with its cut ends immersed in 2.5 cm (1 in.) of water in a glass jar, covered loosely with a plastic bag. It retains good flavour for only a few days.

Serve: Snap the tough basal end off each spear where it breaks naturally. Steam the spears briefly, until barely tender, and serve them with melted butter, hollandaise sauce, or vinaigrette. Dressings that contain vinegar or lemon juice can turn the spears yellow, so add them just before serving.

Preserve: Blanch and freeze the spears.

Suggested Cultivars

'Jersey Giant' is a popular hybrid variety developed by Rutgers University of New Jersey that is reliable, vigorous, disease-resistant and productive on the prairies.

'Guelph Millennium' is a new Canadian hybrid from University of Guelph that tolerates heavier clay soils and cold, wet springs. It has produced well in prairie conditions during the first four years of testing.

Chives

Allium schoenoprasum
Family: onion (*Alliaceae*)
Type: cool-season bulb
Height: 25 to 45 cm (10 to 18 in.)
Space: 25 cm (10 in.)
Light: full sun to part shade
Propagation: division in early spring or fall; seed indoors or outdoors in early spring

The smallest of the onion species, chives are grown for their slender, mild-flavoured leaves that arise from a bulb. Native to Europe and Asia, the plant has been cultivated since the Middle Ages in Europe and for over five thousand years in China.

How to Grow: Seeds germinate readily at room temperature, but the thread-like seedlings grow very slowly and require tedious weeding. Many gardeners begin with a division or a purchased plant.

Chives grow in clumps that look great between other spreading herbs, such as thyme, oregano, and anise hyssop. They bloom profusely in late spring, sporting lavender flowers packed on heads like pompoms. Harvest the flowers before they set seed, to prevent a chive invasion, as it self-sows prolifically. When the leaves turn yellow, rejuvenate the plant by cutting it back to 2.5 cm (1 in.) or divide it when it becomes crowded. Chives die back to underground bulbs in winter and are among the hardiest of the perennial herbs.

Harvest: Snip chive leaves individually to the ground. The blossoms can be plucked as they open.

Chives

Garlic chives

Serve: Minced chives complement many vegetables, especially potatoes. Combined with tarragon, chervil, and parsley, they are one of the essential ingredients of fresh *fines herbes* used to flavour French cuisine. Use the edible flowers to garnish green salads.

Preserve: Unlike other herbs, chives do not dry well, but decent flavour is retained when the leaves are blanched and frozen. The flowers make a mild, onion-scented herbal vinegar.

Related Species

Garlic Chives (*Allium tuberosum*) also grow from clumping bulbs. Their flat leaves and white flowers have a mild garlic flavour, and the flowers are useful as a salad garnish.

Hyssop, Anise

Agastache foeniculum
Family: mint (*Lamiaceae*)
Type: warm-season perennial
Height: 45 to 90 cm (18 to 36 in.)
Space: 45 cm (18 in.)
Light: full sun to partial shade
Propagation: division in spring; seed outdoors after frost date

Anise hyssop, also known as giant hyssop, is a native prairie wildflower with licorice-mint scented foliage and tall, lavender flower spikes. Ornamental and aromatic qualities make this species a delightful addition to any garden, especially if you enjoy herbal tea plants. Its bright green leaves contrast

'Blue Fortune' anise hyssop

nicely against creeping thyme, upright chives, or fuzzy oregano.

How to Grow: Anise hyssop tolerates afternoon shade and flourishes in full sun. Obtain a named cultivar, or sow seeds of the wild species 0.5 cm (0.25 in.) deep directly outdoors after the final spring frost date. Mature plants can be divided in spring as new growth begins. This plant blooms for a long period during summer.

Harvest: Clip leafy stems or pluck leaves and blooms as needed.

Serve: The foliage can be used fresh or dried to make a mild tea. Use the edible flowers as a garnish for salads or desserts.

Preserve: Preserve anise hyssop by drying it.

Suggested Cultivar

'Blue Fortune' forms a compact plant, with pale violet-blue flowers and a sweet anise scent.

Lemon Balm

Melissa officinalis
Family: mint (*Lamiaceae*)
Type: cool-season perennial
Height: 60 cm (2 ft.)
Space: 60 cm (2 ft.)
Light: full sun to shade
Propagation: division in early spring; seed indoors in mid-March, transplant outdoors after frost date

Lemon balm, a plant of southern Europe and North America, is aptly named for its uplifting citrus taste and scent. It has square stems, typical of the mint family, bright green, sparsely hairy leaves with fine scalloped edges, and white or pink flowers that attract bees.

How to Grow: Obtain a division from another plant in early spring. Or, seed indoors in mid-March by pressing the tiny seeds into the soil, but do not completely cover them because light promotes germination. Transplant seedlings outdoors when the plant has at least two sets of true leaves, after the final spring frost date.

Lemon balm will grow in many conditions, but it favours full sun with moist soil. Drought causes the leaves to turn crispy and brown around the edges. Use coarse mulch such as wood chips to retain soil moisture and prevent leaf scorch. It self-sows freely and can spread aggressively; contain it with a physical barrier such as lawn edging or plant it against a sidewalk.

Lemon balm contrasts beautifully against grey sage in a herbal border.

Harvest: Snip sprigs of tender new growth, while carefully handling the leaves, which are easily bruised and discoloured.

Serve: Use fresh lemon balm leaves to flavour fruit salads, poultry dishes, and fish marinades, or steep fresh or dried leaves to make a light herbal tea.

Preserve: Preserve lemon balm by drying it.

Lemon balm

Lovage

Levesticum officinale
Family: parsley (*Apiaceae*)
Type: cool-season perennial
Height: up to 2 m (6.5 ft.)
Space: 2 m (6 ft.)
Light: part shade to full sun
Propagation: division in early spring; moist-chill seeds and seed indoors in early to mid-March or outdoors in early spring, transplant outdoors near frost date

Native to mountainous areas in northern Europe, lovage looks like a giant

Lovage

celery plant as its green shoots emerge in early spring. By mid-summer, it's almost tall enough to provide shade under lacy blossom clusters, which are shaped like flat umbrellas.

How to Grow: Due to its immensity, one lovage plant is usually sufficient. Sow moist-chilled seeds indoors, or outdoors in early spring. The seeds take two to three weeks to sprout at room temperature. Select the strongest seedling and transplant it outdoors near the final spring frost date. To propagate lovage from an existing plant, lift it and take divisions from the outer edge, very early in spring.

Lovage grows best in part shade and moist soil, although it will do well in full sun if it's mulched with a coarse material. Carefully select the planting location, considering the plant's prominent size. It is the largest of the herbs and makes a great backdrop for other perennial plants. Cut lovage back after it blooms to prevent it from becoming rangy and to restrict it from self-sowing seeds in places where you don't want them, but retain some flower heads if you wish to produce seeds. To maintain a vigorous plant, divide it every four years.

Harvest: The young leaves and stalks are most desirable; mature leaves may turn yellow and taste bland. Collect dry seeds in a cloth bag tied over the seed heads to catch them as they shatter. Sow collected seeds immediately or within a year, because their viability decreases rapidly.

Serve: Similar in taste to celery and parsley, lovage leaves and stems are sought after to flavour soups and stews. Lovage leaves mix well with fresh dill, and add zest to potato salad or beans. The leaves are fairly coarse and the stems are fibrous, so they should be finely chopped before using. Use the seeds as seasoning in soups or salad dressings, similar to celery seed.

Preserve: Blanch and freeze lovage leaves. Dried seeds can be stored for one year in a sealed container in a cool, dark cupboard.

Mint
Mentha spp.
Family: mint (*Lamiaceae*)
Type: cool-season perennial
Height: 30 to 90 cm (1 to 3 ft.)
Space: 45 cm (18 in.)
Light: full sun to shade
Propagation: division in spring

Mint was named after Minthe, a nymph of Greek mythology who was transformed into a sweet-smelling plant. The origins of some mint species are unknown, but many are native to Europe. Hundreds of cultivated varieties exist, with common names that describe their particular scent or flavour; apple, pineapple, orange,

Spearmint

chocolate, and ginger mint are just a few. The aromatic oils are emitted from resinous spots on the stems and leaves, and fragrance varies tremendously between varieties. Square stems are characteristic of mints, as well as dense flower spikes that attract bees.

How to Grow: Mints readily hybridize with each other naturally, so you can wind up with a patchwork of unpredictable characteristics in plants that are grown from seed. It is better to obtain named cultivars with known desirable scents. Plant mint outdoors, after the final spring frost date.

Depending on your growing conditions and the species, mint can get quite tall and it spreads aggressively. It will quickly colonize a shady or sunny space and should be contained by a physical barrier such as a large, deep plastic pot with the bottom cut off. Sink the pot in the garden so the rim is level with the soil surface, and hidden by mulch. Rejuvenate lanky plants by cutting them back by two-thirds. All mints, including tender species, can be enjoyed as potted plants, but even the hardiest species will not survive prairie winters in a container. Overwinter hardy container-grown plants by transplanting them or sinking the entire pot into the garden in autumn, at least six weeks before the ground freezes.

Harvest: Snip sprigs or leaves from new growth.

Serve: Fresh mint is the ultimate garnish for ice-cold summer drinks. It also goes well with peas and makes a tasty jelly. Brew fresh or dried mint into a refreshing tea, or use it to impart its characteristic flavour to Mediterranean dishes such as *tabouleh*.

Preserve: Preserve mint by drying it.

Suggested Cultivars
Ginger mint (*Mentha arvensis* 'Variegata') has gold-flecked leaves and a faint ginger aroma.

Peppermint (*Mentha piperita*) is a popular mint with dark green foliage and a strong menthol flavour.

Spearmint (*Mentha spicata*) is the most common hardy mint, with large leaves and a sweet scent and taste.

Oregano, Greek
Origanum vulgare ssp. *hirtum*
Family: mint (*Lamiaceae*)
Type: warm-season perennial
Height: 30 to 60 cm (1 to 2 ft.)
Space: 45 cm (18 in.)
Light: full sun
Propagation: division in spring; seed indoors in mid-March, transplant outdoors after the frost date

Native to the Mediterranean, oregano forms a creeping mound of soft, fuzzy, deep green leaves. Common or wild oregano has pink flowers, while the preferred Greek variety has white flowers. Confusion exists over the identity

Greek oregano

and naming of this plant, and there are numerous cultivars.

How to grow: Seed indoors by pressing the tiny seeds into the soil, but do not cover them completely as light promotes germination. Transplant seedlings outdoors after the danger of frost has passed. Mature plants can be divided just as the plant begins to sprout in spring.

Plant oregano in a hot, sunny location, where the soil has excellent drainage. It grows best if the soil becomes fairly dry between irrigations. After the plant blooms, cut it back to 10 cm (4 in.) to maintain a neat shape. Its low-growing form and dark green foliage stand out against upright herbs such as chives and tarragon.

Oregano survives winter in some areas if the site is well drained, but in places where it is marginal, it should be protected with mulch.

Harvest: Snip sprigs of new growth. Oregano's flavour is strongest just as flower buds begin to form, but before they open.

Serve: Oregano is a classic seasoning for tomato sauce and pizza. It is also the essential herb for Greek salads of chopped cucumbers, tomatoes, onions, olives, and feta cheese, dressed with lemon juice, garlic, and olive oil.

Preserve: Drying enhances oregano's flavour.

Suggested Cultivars

Greek oregano (*Origanum vulgare* ssp. *hirtum* or *Origanum heracleoticum*) is considered the best culinary cultivar. Common oregano (*Origanum vulgare* ssp. *vulgare*) lacks the distinctive flavour treasured in Greek and Italian cuisine.

Golden oregano (*Origanum vulgare* 'Aureum') is an ornamental cultivar with a golden cast to its leaves and a subtle, mild flavour.

Raspberry
Rubus spp.
Family: rose (*Rosaceae*)
Type: cool-season perennial with biennial stems
Height: 1 to 1.5m (3 to 5 ft.)

Space: 45 to 90 cm (18 to 36 in.)
Light: full sun, except 'Honeyqueen,' which tolerates partial shade
Pollination: self-fruitful, only one cultivar is necessary
Propagation: bare-root crowns in early May; division in early spring

Resembling faceted ruby jewels, ripe raspberries are one of summer's most precious fruits. The prickly plants grow wild in cool woods in North America, Europe and Asia, and were first cultivated in Europe during the 1500s. While the plant is not particularly ornamental, its fragile, scrumptious berries justify space in your garden.

Raspberry roots are perennial, but they produce biennial stems called canes, which die after fruiting. Depending on the cultivar, the main crop is either produced on one-year old canes known as "primocanes," or two-year old stems called "floricanes."

Most prairie-hardy raspberry cultivars bear fruit on floricanes, and are known as "summer-bearing" types. These produce heavy crops with fairly uniform ripening, generally in late July and early August. Each spring, the plant sprouts green primocanes. During the season, these canes initiate flower buds, develop a protective brown bark, and then overwinter as dormant, bare stems. The following spring, the same canes bloom and produce fruit. New canes sprout every season to continue the cycle.

A second type, called "fall-bearing" (or "everbearing"), produces fruit on the tips of the primocanes in late summer. However, the canes require much of the growing season to become sufficiently developed to bear fruit, so ripening is usually a race against frost. In regions with hot summers, the harvest begins in mid to late August and lasts into September. In many areas, the growing season isn't warm enough or long enough to get a satisfactory crop. Primocane types don't yield as much as floricane types, but they extend the season with very sweet, late berries.

How to Grow: Raspberry plants are self-fruitful; only one cultivar is needed to produce fruit. It's best to obtain disease-free, nursery-grown stock of a named cultivar.

This thorny crop is easiest to manage if you isolate it in a bed with access via a path or stepping-stones for berry picking. The plants can serve as a backdrop to a separate border of low-growing edibles. Choose a site with well-drained soil and amend it with plenty of organic matter. Avoid planting raspberries in low areas where frost can damage early blossoms or late-season fruit.

Raspberries are usually cultivated in a row and supported by a trellis. A simple trellis consists of a stake at each end of the row, with two lengths of wire or strong twine strung between the stakes. The wire surrounds the canes, holding them upright, so they

'Double Delight' raspberries

receive sunlight and air circulation, while keeping the fruit clean and easy to pick. Staking the plants also reduces damage to the canes from wind whipping. Begin with at least five plants to eventually fill a 3 m (10 ft.) row.

Raspberries can also be grown in a large clump, with five canes planted around and tied to a central stake. Allow about 45 cm (18 in.) between plants and 1.5 m (5 ft.) between clumps.

Raspberries are planted in early spring before the plants leaf out, usually in late April to early May. At this time garden centres and seed catalogues supply bare-root crowns, which must be planted immediately. Keep bare-root plants in a bucket of water in the shade while you prepare the planting holes. Raspberries are planted so that the crown, where the stem meets the root, is situated at or just beneath the soil surface. After planting, trim the cane to 15 cm (6 in.).

Once the initial planting becomes established, your raspberry patch can be expanded with divisions taken in early spring. The easiest method is to separate suckers from an existing mother plant. Plant divisions or suckers in the same manner as bare-root stock. Container-grown plants can be installed during the growing season, until mid-September.

Most raspberry cultivars sucker profusely and rapidly spread out of bounds. Suckers arise from roots

within the top 25 cm (10 in.) of soil, and can be restrained by sinking a board 30 cm (12 in.) into the ground as a barrier. Place the board parallel to the row, about 30 to 45 cm (12 to 18 in.) out from the plants, to keep the patch within reasonable reach for maintenance and harvesting.

Raspberries are shallow-rooted and require weekly watering throughout the growing season, but reduce irrigation in late summer after the hot weather dissipates to allow the plants to harden off. Soak the soil again thoroughly in late fall, just before the ground freezes. In very exposed areas, young canes can be protected from winter desiccation by bending them to the ground and covering them with a board and 10 cm (4 in.) of soil. Uncover them in early spring before the buds break.

Raspberry canes are removed after they bear fruit, but on the prairies it's helpful to leave them in place to trap mulch and snow during winter. In March, cut them to the ground and discard them. The old, spent floricanes can be distinguished by their dry, shrivelled, light-coloured appearance. Thin the remaining productive canes to 15 cm (6 in.) apart, keeping the healthiest, thickest stems for your new crop.

Fall-bearing primocane types are usually managed by cutting all the canes completely down to the ground in late winter. The tips of these canes will appear shrivelled where fruit was borne, while the lower portion may have live foliage and flower buds. If left to grow, the buds can develop a bonus crop, but it diverts energy from growing new stems and producing the main crop.

Raspberries are troubled by caterpillars of the raspberry sawfly and the raspberry crown borer. The sawfly caterpillar can defoliate plants. If holes appear in the leaves in spring and summer, check the undersides for small sawfly larvae with white spiny bristles, and if found, pick them off and squish them.

The adult crown borer is a moth that mimics a yellow-jacket wasp; its offspring look like white grubs and they feed on raspberry crowns and destroy new shoots. The female lays eggs on the undersides of raspberry leaves in late August, and the larvae hatch in October and burrow into the crown. In spring the larvae tunnel into the canes and cause the stem to swell and form galls near the soil line. To control the damage caused by this pest, remove and destroy wilted canes and those with swellings at the base.

Harvest: Pick raspberries when they change colour completely and easily slip off the fruit core, which remains attached to the plant. Collect the berries in shallow, covered containers to keep them intact and firm, and chill them immediately. Raspberries keep only a few days.

Serve: Raspberries taste fabulous fresh, or in baking, ice cream, fruit shakes, or jam.

Preserve: Simply freeze whole berries or make them into jam. The 'Honeyqueen' cultivar does not freeze well.

Suggested Cultivars
Summer-bearing floricanes
'Boyne' is a productive, early season variety with slightly tart fruit, introduced by the Morden Research Centre in 1960. It's the standard hardy floricane by which others are judged. It has vigorous, self-supporting canes and suckers freely, but is not as disease-resistant as newer varieties.

'Honeyqueen' was bred by Robert Erskine of Rocky Mountain House, Alberta. It is a very hardy and disease-resistant, mid-season floricane that can be grown in partial shade. It produces golden yellow, mild-flavoured fruit.

'SK Red Mammoth' was released in 1999 from the University of Saskatchewan. It produces vigorous, disease-resistant floricanes that require support. It's slightly hardier than 'Boyne' and bears sweet, large fruit.

'SK Steadfast' is a University of Saskatchewan release with fruit that is similar to 'Boyne.' The floricanes produce lower yields than 'Boyne,' but the plant is hardier and disease-resistant. It is non-suckering and therefore recommended for small urban gardens.

Fall-bearing primocanes

'Double Delight' is a hardy Morden Research Centre primocane release with excellent flavour. It grows to about 1.5 m (5 ft.), and produces ripe fruit from mid-August until frost.

'Red River' is a hardy primocane from Morden Research Centre with short 1.1 m (3.5 ft.) canes. It bears smaller fruit than 'Double Delight' and produces about a week earlier.

Rhubarb

Rheum rhabarbarum
Family: buckwheat (*Polygonaceae*)
Type: cool-season perennial
Height: 1 m (3 ft.)
Space: 1 to 1.2 m (3 to 4 ft.)
Light: full sun

Propagation: division in early spring

With origins in southern Siberia, it's not surprising that rhubarb is extremely hardy. It's also very tart, and its popularity as a food plant increased when sugar became widely available in the seventeenth century. Rhubarb provides the earliest dessert ingredient from the garden. The red leaf stem is the edible portion; the leaves contain toxic compounds and should never be eaten.

Rhubarb makes a dramatic entrance as its huge leaves unfurl in early spring. Striking crimson stalks and enormous foliage qualify it as a feature plant, and it combines well with finer-leaved spreading herbs such as tarragon and thyme. Cool temperatures can enhance the red coloration, although cultivars with muted colour are often more vigorous and just as tasty.

How to Grow: Plant rhubarb in early spring from a potted plant or a division. Divisions are obtained from an established plant by lifting it and separating or cutting off sections with at least one bud. Set the crown, where the shoot meets the root, about 5 cm (2 in.) beneath the soil surface. One plant is sufficient for a small urban garden, although rhubarb fans might like more.

Flowering stalks should be removed if they appear, as seed production requires energy and rhubarb is propagated through division. After the first frost, remove and compost the spent plant remains, and dispose of any diseased plant parts. If fungal leaf spots occur (small yellow areas that become white spots with red margins), remove and destroy the infected leaves promptly to control the disease. Aphids transfer this disease; in severe infections the leaves droop and the crown eventually dies. Keep your rhubarb plant vigorous by dividing it when the stems become crowded and less robust, about every six years.

Harvest: Refrain from harvesting the first year after planting, to produce a strong plant. Pick a single sampling of stems in the second year. From the third year on, the leaf stalks can be harvested from late May until early July, taking no more than one-third of the plant at a time. To avoid introducing decay organisms into the plant, pull the stalks, rather than cutting them. Grasp the base of the stalk and pull it straight up and out of the plant. It should separate easily from the clump. Cut the leaf off the stalk immediately to prevent wilt. The leaves can be composted; the inedible compounds in the leaves will not affect your compost.

Rinse rhubarb stalks and dry them immediately before refrigerating them. The stalks will swell and split if left to soak.

Serve: Rhubarb is usually stewed with sugar, or used in desserts and pies, often combined with strawberries. To make a refreshing summer punch, strain the syrup from stewed, sweetened rhubarb and pour it over ice with a splash of ginger ale.

Preserve: Simply chop the stalks into 2.5 cm (1 in.) pieces and freeze them, or make rhubarb jam.

Suggested Cultivars

'Canada Red' is a popular variety with a vigorous growth pattern. It produces medium red stems and few seed stalks.

'Honey Red' was introduced in 1971 by A. J. (Bert) Porter of Honeywood Nursery in Saskatchewan. It produces sweet, deep red stems with few seed stalks.

'MacDonald' is a very vigorous, productive plant with large red, sweet stalks, developed at MacDonald Agricultural College in Quebec.

'Canada Red' rhubarb

'Valentine' produces very sweet and long, bright red stems with few seed stalks, but it is less vigorous than other cultivars. Its stems retain good colour when cooked.

Sage

Salvia officinalis
Family: mint (*Lamiaceae*)
Type: cool-season perennial
Height: 45 cm (18 in.)
Space: 45 cm (18 in.)
Light: full sun or partial shade
Propagation: seed indoors in mid-March, transplant outdoors near frost date

Originally from southern Europe, sage is a potent, spicy herb. Its scientific

Sage

name, *Salvia*, comes from the Latin "to heal," and the plant has a history of various medicinal uses. Sage grows to become a small shrubby plant with fragrant, grey-green, pebbly-textured leaves and blooms in early summer. Its blossoms are usually pale violet, but some plants have pink or white flowers. Cultivated varieties with golden, purple, or variegated leaves are not as hardy as the common gray culinary species.

How to Grow: Seed indoors, 0.5 cm (0.25 in.) deep, in mid-March and transplant seedlings outdoors near the frost date. Although sage is slow to sprout, the seedlings grow quickly.

Sage requires well-drained soil and is very drought-tolerant. The plant grows best in full sun and becomes less compact when grown in partial shade. It looks quite attractive when combined with any cultivar of thyme, planted at its base.

Trim sage to rejuvenate and shape the plant or to remove winter-damaged stems. It tolerates pruning into woody growth.

Harvest: Snip or pluck young leaves from the tips of the plant.

Serve: A touch of sage is indispensable in poultry stuffing, mixed with onion, celery, carrots, parsley, and breadcrumbs. It also goes well with sausage and other meats and cheeses. Steep fresh sage sprigs in hot water with sugar to make an intensely fragrant tea in the Middle Eastern style. Its spicy flavour is powerful, so use it sparingly.

Preserve: Dried sage retains excellent flavour.

Sorrel, French
Rumex scutatus
Family: buckwheat (*Polygonaceae*)
Type: cool-season perennial
Height: 20 to 30 cm (8 to 12 in.)
Space: 30 cm (1 ft.)
Light: part shade to full sun
Propagation: division in early spring or fall; seed indoors in mid-March, transplant outdoors near frost date

Native to Europe and Asia, French sorrel rapidly forms a perennial clump of arrow- or fiddle-shaped leaves. Its name originates from old French for "sour" as this herb imparts a tangy taste. Sorrel was gathered wild until French gardeners brought it under cultivation in the late 1600s. Its zesty flavour is essential to the classic French sorrel soup. Another species that is cultivated for the same purpose is the large-leaved common garden sorrel (*Rumex acetosa*).

How to Grow: Obtain a division or a plant of a named cultivar, or seed indoors, 1 cm (0.5 in.) deep, in mid-March. Transplant seedlings outdoors near the frost date.

Sorrel is an attractive plant for the perennial border, although some varieties have the potential to become invasive. Creeping cultivars can be

'Blonde De Lyon' sorrel

contained in a 30 cm (12 in.) deep bottomless pot, sunk in the garden, so that the rim of the pot is level with the soil surface. Cultivars that do not produce seed are most desirable. If a flower stalk appears, snip it off to prevent the plant from self-sowing. Rejuvenate the plant by removing older, outer leaves to promote new growth at the centre.

Harvest: Pluck sorrel leaves for fresh use from the outer edges of the plant. The leaf quality is best in early spring, and it diminishes in summer as leaves become tough.

Serve: Young French sorrel leaves are mild enough to use as an accent in salads. The larger leaves of common garden sorrel are best for soups. Oxalic acid is responsible for the herb's lemony zest, but it is unhealthy when eaten raw in large quantities. Heat neutralizes the toxicity, although the cooking time should be minimal to preserve the herb's flavour. Use a stainless steel pot, not cast iron or aluminum, so the acidic leaves do not pick up a metallic taste.

Preserve: Blanch the leaves and freeze them.

Suggested Cultivars
'Profusion' is a patented cultivar, selected from a natural mutation in France, and introduced commercially by Richter's Herbs in 1993.

It is succulent, doesn't produce seeds, and can be used as a salad or soup herb.

'Blonde de Lyon' is a garden sorrel that rarely produces seed stalks. It features large, thick, slightly acidic leaves.

Strawberry
Fragaria x *ananassa*
Family: rose (*Rosaceae*)
Type: cool-season perennial
Height: less than 15 cm (6 in.)
Space: 30 cm (12 in.) for day neutral and ever-bearing types, 45 cm (18 in.) for June-bearing types
Light: full sun
Pollination: self-fruitful; only one cultivar is necessary

The light perfume and luscious flavour of ripe, red strawberries is an unforgettable summer experience: even their botanical name is based on the Latin *fragrans* or "odorous," referring to the sweetly scented fruit. Wild strawberries are known to have been collected for millennia. Modern garden strawberries were developed in Europe in the 1750s from a hybrid between two wild strawberries of the Americas: the large-fruited strawberry (*Fragaria chiloensis*) that grows along the Pacific Coast from Alaska to Chile, and a tiny, aromatic strawberry (*Fragaria virginiana*) that is native across the prairies and throughout eastern North America.

There are three types of strawberries, determined by when the plants

'Tristar' strawberries

set flower buds and produce fruit: June-bearing, day-neutral, and ever-bearing. Most berries grown on the prairies are June-bearing or day-neutral types.

Strawberry season opens with berries from June-bearing plants (usually in early July on the prairies). Short days in late summer trigger this type to initiate flower buds, but the plants don't bloom until the following season, so the first harvest occurs the year after planting. After that, a crop is borne each year. June-bearing types yield the most, producing a single, heavy crop that ripens over three weeks. This type is superb for making jam, since a large quantity of fruit is available within a short period.

Day-neutral strawberries bloom as soon as the plants become rooted, regardless of the day length, and produce a steady supply of berries until frost. Flowering typically begins mid-June and fruiting occurs in mid-July, with the heaviest berry production in August and September, although blossoming diminishes during peak summer heat. Some gardeners treat day-neutral strawberries like annual plants and replant them every year, which eliminates the need to over-winter plants.

A third type, called the "ever-bearing" strawberry bears two crops. The first crop develops the year after planting, from flower buds produced the previous summer and it overlaps with June-bearing types. A second crop is initiated during the current growing season and ripens in late summer, usually September. Ever-bearing varieties

such as 'Fort Laramie' and 'Ogallala' were once popular for their second crop, but have been largely replaced by the day-neutral cultivars. Occasionally, garden centres and seed catalogues incorrectly label day-neutral cultivars as "ever-bearing."

Strawberry plants are quite pretty throughout the growing season, and their dark green, low-growing rosettes make versatile landscape companions. As an alternative to growing them in a bed, use them as a groundcover, to fill a large container, or tuck them among edible flowers and herbs in the front of a border.

How to Grow: Plant strawberries from late April to the beginning of May, when bare-root one-year-old plants are available from garden centres or seed catalogues. These must be planted immediately. Only one cultivar is necessary to obtain fruit. Choose a sunny location with well-drained soil that contains plenty of organic matter, and avoid planting in low spots where frost pockets occur.

For a satisfactory harvest, start with at least two dozen plants, which will fill an area that is 1.2 m (4 ft.) wide and 1.5 m (5 ft.) long. Keep the plants cool and moist, wrapped in damp cloth or paper in plastic bags in the refrigerator, while you prepare the planting area. Dig the planting hole large enough for the roots to completely extend down and out, and position the mid-point of the crown

(the short stem between the leaves and roots) level with the soil surface. If it is buried too deep, the plant will rot, and if too shallow, the plant will dry out, as most of the roots are in the top 15 cm (6 in.) of soil.

To establish strong plants, remove flower buds that develop on day-neutral plants the first six weeks after planting and on June-bearing or ever-bearing plants during the entire first season.

Strawberries need even soil moisture throughout the growing season, and should be mulched to retain moisture, reduce weed competition and to keep the fruit clean. Traditionally, home garden plants are mulched with straw, but wood chips can also be used. Plastic mulch is suitable for day-neutral types, but it prevents June-bearing runners from rooting. Reduce watering in late summer to allow plants to harden off, then soak the soil deeply in late fall before it freezes.

June-bearing varieties should be trimmed back to 5 cm (2 in.) after the fruit crop is harvested, taking care not to cut the developing new leaves. The mother plant will generate new plants on long stems called runners. Encourage runner plants to root by pressing the base slightly into the soil, while retaining a 15 cm (6 in.) space between plants. Rejuvenate the June-bearing patch each year this way, removing old mother plants. Day-neutral and ever-bearing strawberries do not need to be trimmed; these types expend energy, yielding berries all season, and develop few runners.

Keep the strawberries free of weeds and fruit debris, and remove and destroy any diseased plant parts, particularly those with fuzzy grey mould. To maintain good production and healthy plants, replace your strawberry patch entirely with new plants every three years, and move it to a new location. Avoid planting it in the same place where vegetables in the nightshade family (tomatoes, peppers, potatoes, and eggplant) have been grown in the past two years, because these crops can harbour fungal diseases that remain in the soil and affect strawberries.

Protect strawberries from winter damage with organic mulch such as weed-free straw or shredded leaves, about 10 to 15 cm (4 to 6 in.) deep. Apply the mulch after a few hard frosts in late October or early November. Uncover the plant crown in early spring as active growth begins, and use the mulch between the plants to retain moisture and suppress weeds.

Harvest: Strawberries will continue to increase in size as the berry changes colour. Pick the fruit when it is completely red and not showing any white, with the green cap and stem attached. Chill the berries in a covered container immediately after picking; the fruit keeps only a few days. Cool weather delays ripening, while hot weather accelerates it. Misshapen berries occur

when flowers are only partially pollinated, but odd shapes are cosmetic and do not affect flavour.

Serve: Enjoy juicy fresh strawberries, or use them in pastries and baking, jam, ice cream, and shakes.

Preserve: Freeze whole berries or preserve them by making fruit leather or jam.

Suggested Cultivars
June-bearing
'Kent' is the most popular and productive June-bearing strawberry grown on the prairies. It was developed at the Agriculture and Agri-Food Canada research station in Kentville, Nova Scotia. It's very hardy, and yields very large, quality berries with good flavour, and abundant runners. It's slightly susceptible to mildew.

Day neutral
'Fern' is hardy and produces sweet-flavoured medium-size berries. This variety bears earlier than 'Tristar,' although it is less commonly available.

'Seascape' is a hardy release from University of California at Davis that produces large, quality berries. The plant is very productive, but slightly susceptible to mildew.

'Tristar' is a very popular day-neutral variety that produces medium-size berries with intense flavour. It bears late in the season and continues until frost. The plant is quite hardy and disease-resistant.

Tarragon, French

Artemisia dracunculus var. *sativa*
Family: sunflower (*Asteraceae*)
Type: cool-season perennial
Height: 75 cm (30 in.)
Space: 60 cm (2 ft.)
Light: full sun to part shade
Propagation: division in early spring

Tarragon originates from southern Europe and Asia, and has been cultivated for over two thousand years. It is related to a group of fragrant plants that are native to the prairies, including sagebrush (*Artemisia cana*) and prairie sage (*Artemisia frigida*).

Tarragon features slender, light grey-green leaves with a yellowish tinge on wiry stems that proliferate into a bushy plant. The French variety *sativa* has aromatic leaves and the preferred flavour, similar to anise or licorice. It rarely produces seed and is propagated by division. Russian tarragon (simply identified as *Artemisia dracunculus* with no variety name) is a larger, hardier plant, which produces seed, but has little flavour and is considered inferior for culinary purposes.

How to Grow: Plant tarragon from a division in early spring or a potted plant. It grows in a wide range of conditions. Tarragon grows rapidly and can look straggly by midsummer; rejuvenate the plant by cutting it back to 15 cm (6 in.). At the end of the growing season, allow the stems to remain in place to trap snow, and cut them back to the ground the following spring.

Harvest: Clip leafy stems for fresh use; young leaves have the best flavour.

Serve: French tarragon makes fine salad dressings and vinegars, and it complements the flavour of light meats such as chicken and fish. It is also one herb component of the fresh *fines herbes* used in French cuisine.

Preserve: Tarragon's flavour diminishes significantly when it is dried, so it is better to preserve the taste by steeping leaf sprigs in vinegar, and using the vinegar in dressings. Alternately, blanch the leafy stems and freeze them.

French tarragon

Thyme

Thymus spp.
Family: mint (*Lamiaceae*)
Type: cool-season perennial
Height: varies, up to 30 cm (1 ft.)
Space: 45 cm (18 in.)
Light: full sun
Propagation: division in early spring

Thyme encompasses a few hundred species of aromatic low-growing perennial plants from Europe and Asia. Its name is derived from the Greek *thyo* "to perfume." Like mints, thymes hybridize readily with each other, and there is much confusion regarding names, even among experts. This leads to problems with identification and in determining which ones are hardy, so it's best to obtain your plants as divisions or as a purchased plant that is known to be hardy and fragrant.

Non-hardy varieties can be enjoyed as potted plants.

Some thymes grow slightly upright and become semi-woody, while others remain soft and green and creep absolutely flat along the ground, spilling over rocks. All have plant parts that are scaled-down to a diminutive level: the stems are wiry, and the leaves, flowers, and seeds are tiny. Thyme is excellent for edging beds and pathways, or forming a carpet between stepping-stones, although it does not hold up well to trampling. In spring, thyme blossoms form a dazzling mat of bright pink, white, or lavender flowers.

How to Grow: Most thymes are propagated by dividing existing plants where they naturally root along the ground. Simply lift the plant and separate a

Lemon thyme

rooted section, or encourage root-ing by pressing the plant into contact with the soil. Replant rooted sections in early spring. Keep plant divisions moist until the root system anchors the plant and new growth appears.

Thyme requires full sun and excellent drainage. It may die back in sections, and can be rejuvenated by cutting back ragged growth in mid-summer, but avoid cutting into woody stems, except to remove dead ones.

Harvest: Harvest short, leafy sprigs for fresh use.

Serve: Use chopped fresh thyme, or crumbled dried thyme in a wide range of vegetarian and meat dishes. It com-bines well with lemon as a seasoning for poultry.

Preserve: Dried thyme retains good flavour.

HERBAL VINEGAR

Vinegar is a fine base to capture the essence of fresh herbs in order to in-fuse a salad dressing or marinade with flavour. Rinse and dry your choice herbs, place them in a glass container with an acid-resistant cap (canning jars work well), and cover the herbs with plain white vinegar. Close the lid and place the mix in a dark place at room temperature for four weeks. Strain to remove the herbs and decant the herbal vinegar into a glass container, and store it at room temperature. Tarragon produces a classic herbal vinegar, while chive blossoms produce a lovely rose-tinted one.

HERBAL TEA

Brewing herbal tea is an art, guided by your taste buds. Begin with several stems or a handful of fresh leaves in a pot, and pour boiling water over them. Steep for about five minutes, and sweeten if desired. When using dried herbs, use about one teaspoon per cup. Mint and lemon balm are most popular, but other herbs can be used to make delicious blends. For refreshing summer drinks, chill the tea after brewing and garnish with a fresh stem of the herb used.

Suggested Cultivars

English or garden thyme (*Thymus vulgaris*) is among the most popular culinary species, but it does not overwinter as well as the species known as mother-of-thyme or creeping thyme (*Thymus serpyllum*). Both species have culinary value.

Lemon thyme (*Thymus* x *citriodorus*) is known to over-winter in Chinook areas of the prairies; it has dark green foliage that may be edged with yellow margins and it produces a superb lemon fragrance.

Silver lemon thyme (*Thymus* x *citriodorus* 'Argenteus') has a variegated green leaf with silver edging and a citrus fragrance.

Fruiting Shrubs and Fruit Trees
Apple

Malus spp.

Family: rose (*Rosaceae*)
Type: deciduous tree
Height: depends on variety and rootstock, 4 to 6 m (13 to 20 ft.); dwarf 2 m (7 ft.)
Space: 4 to 6 m (13 to 20 ft.); dwarf 2 to 3 m (7 to 10 ft.)
Light: full sun
Pollination: cross-pollinated; plant two different apple cultivars or an apple and a crabapple

Crisp, juicy apples are a cherished symbol of autumn, generated from a blanket of beautiful blossoms on the most popular fruit tree in prairie gardens. Our choice of apple cultivars is due to breeding efforts that began with horticultural pioneers like William Saunders, the first director of the Dominion Experimental Farm in Ottawa. In the 1880s Saunders bred standard apple varieties with the Siberian crabapple (*Malus baccata*), in a quest for worthy fruit that would survive prairie conditions. Contemporary varieties such as 'September Ruby,' 'Norkent,' and 'Prairie Magic' share their lineage with this tiny crabapple, the hardiest of apples. Cecil Patterson continued work with Saunders's apples and other fruits, when he launched the prairie fruit-breeding program at the University of Saskatchewan in the 1920s. Today, the program perseveres, breeding prairie-hardy fruits to satisfy our appetites.

Apple cultivars are divided into groups depending on when the fruit is ready to harvest. The season begins with early varieties that ripen in mid-August to early September, followed by mid-season apples during September and late season cultivars in late September through October.

Apple trees are also classified by size. Commercial growers determine tree size by measuring caliper (the diameter of the trunk at a specified height), but garden literature and retail operations usually describe apple trees in terms of height. Prairie-hardy cultivars tend to fall in the "semi-dwarf" category of trees that reach between 3 to 4.5 m (10 to 15 ft.). Taller trees are referred to as "standard," and shorter trees are termed "dwarf." A tree can be further reduced in size by grafting it on a dwarfing rootstock. Dwarfing rootstocks limit the tree size without affecting the fruit size or characteristics.

Larger trees are suitable for ornamental purposes, shade or screening, but if fruit production is your goal, choose a dwarf tree. It's easier to prune and thin a tree when its branches are within reach and these practices are necessary to produce quality fruit. In addition to being the ideal size for small urban lots, dwarf trees begin bearing at a younger age and are more convenient to harvest than their taller counterparts.

Many prairie-hardy cultivars are available as dwarf trees. The trees are reduced in size by grafting them on hardy dwarfing rootstocks known as 'Ottawa 3' and 'Bud 9,' and research to further reduce tree size is likely to result in "super-dwarfing" rootstocks in the near future.

How to Grow: Choose two different apple cultivars with overlapping blossom periods so that each will have adequate cross-pollination for fruiting. Early and late season cultivars will not likely sufficiently overlap with each other, although both might overlap with a mid-season cultivar. Some crabapples will effectively pollinate apples, but better pollination takes place with other apples. Insects can

carry pollen from a neighbour's tree if it is within 150 m (500 ft.).

It takes several years for apple trees to reach maturity and bear fruit, and this development period is determined by the cultivar and rootstock. The fruit is produced on short, stubby spurs that form on wood that is two years old and older. Fruiting spurs are long-lived and should be handled with care during thinning and harvesting.

Thinning is the best way to increase the size of your apples. In addition, thinning each year helps overcome the biennial bearing habit that some apple cultivars possess, where the tree alternates between producing a heavy crop one year and no fruit the next year. Details for thinning and pruning fruits are provided in Chapter 3. Prune an apple tree yearly to open the tree up to sunlight and air circulation, and aim to keep branches with wide angles that grow almost horizontal, as these are stronger and fruit better than upright ones.

The cultivars listed here produce all-purpose apples that are good for fresh eating and cooking. It is also noted if the cultivar is especially suited for other purposes such as dehydrating or juicing.

Harvest: As the fruit matures, the skin changes colour, the seeds turn brown, and the flesh becomes sweeter. When ripe, the apple stem should separate from the woody spur on the tree easily. Pick an apple by supporting it in one hand while gently twisting the stem off the spur with the other hand. Take care not to drop or bruise the fruit.

Serve: Apples are a terrific fresh snack, and make fabulous pies and desserts. The fruit is versatile for baking, making fruit leather, juice, and applesauce. Late season apples store best, and may keep for months if refrigerated.

Preserve: Core and slice apples, then freeze the slices or dry them in a food dehydrator. Before dehydrating, toss the slices with lemon juice to reduce browning.

Suggested Cultivars
Early

'Norland' originated at the Morden Research Station, and was selected at the Experimental Farm in Scott, Saskatchewan. It was released in 1979 through the Prairie Cooperative Fruit Breeding Program. This upright spreading tree bears small greenish-yellow fruit, striped with red. Although it is moderately susceptible to fire blight, it is a reliable producer and one of the hardiest apples. The fruit has a relatively short shelf life, but will store about 2 months if picked before fully ripe.

'SK Prairie Sun' is a 1999 release, bred by Rick Sawatsky at the University of Saskatchewan. The tree is very hardy, resistant to fire blight, and is naturally semi-dwarf. It bears

'Gemini' apples. PHOTO - JEFFRIES NURSERY

yellowish-cream fruit blushed with pink and the flesh resists browning so this cultivar makes excellent dried apples. It stores about six weeks.

Mid-season

'Carlos Queen' was bred by Robert Erskine of Rocky Mountain House, Alberta. The tree is moderately hardy and has a strong branching habit, although it is susceptible to fire blight. The apples are pale green, blushed with gold with flesh

'Haralson' apple blossoms

that resists oxidation. The fruit is excellent fresh and for cooking. It stores about eight weeks.

'Fall Red' is a very hardy variety that originated from the Morden Research Station, was selected at the University of Alberta, and introduced in 1986 through the Prairie Cooperative Fruit Breeding Program. It has moderate resistance to fire blight and a biennial bearing habit. Its large, dark red apples are good for juicing and store well.

'Gemini' is a new, very hardy release from Art Coutts, a Unity, Saskatchewan, grower. It is similar to 'Goodland,' but hardier and produces good yields of large fruit with an excellent storage life.

'Goodland' is a popular, moderately hardy apple developed at the Morden Research Station. Selected in 1925, and named in 1955, its fruit is light green, washed with red. It is moderately resistant to fire blight, has good yields, and stores fairly well.

'Norkent' is a very hardy selection that originated at the Morden Research Station and was selected by the University of Alberta and Beaverlodge Research Station. Named in 1990, it was never officially released. The tree has a sturdy structure and moderate disease resistance. It produces large, light green- and red-streaked apples that taste similar to 'Golden Delicious' if allowed to fully ripen, and is a good juicing apple. The shelf life is over three months.

'Prairie Magic' is a very hardy selection made by Wilfred Drysdale, a grower in Neepawa, Manitoba. It is similar to 'Goodland,' but hardier and sweeter. It is a consistent annual bearer with moderate disease resistance. It produces pale green apples with a red blush. Released in 2001, royalties from the purchase of this tree go toward a prairie horticulture scholarship.

'Prairie Sensation' is a 2007 very hardy release from University of Saskatchewan. On a dwarfing rootstock, it can produce fruit within two to three years. The fruit is of dessert quality, crisp and juicy, similar to a 'Gala,' only larger, and it stores well.

'September Ruby' is a very hardy annual bearer with bright red, quality all-purpose apples that also make good juice and store well. It is a popular cultivar, although it has been found to be susceptible to fire blight. It originated at the Morden Research Station and was selected at the Beaverlodge Research Station, then introduced through the Prairie Cooperative Fruit Breeding Program in 1986.

Late

'Haralson' is considered moderately hardy, because the fruit ripens too late for zone 2, even though the tree is very hardy. Introduced by the University of Minnesota in 1923, it is a small, strong tree with moderate resistance to fire blight and a biennial bearing habit. It produces large red and creamy-yellow apples with an excellent storage life. The fruit makes good fresh eating if it has enough time to mature.

'Minnesota 447' is a moderately hardy 1950s introduction from University of Minnesota. It is a sturdy tree with moderate disease resistance. The apples are red with yellow streaks and are excellent fresh, and for making sauce and juice. The fruit has an excellent storage life.

Cherry, Dwarf Sour

Prunus x *kerrasis*
Family: rose (*Rosaceae*)
Type: large deciduous shrub
Height: 2 to 2.5 m (6.5 to 8 ft.)
Space: 2 to 3 m (6.5 to 10 ft.)
Light: full sun
Pollination: self-fruitful, only one plant is necessary

Recently introduced by the University of Saskatchewan, dwarf sour cherries are gaining recognition as the most desirable fruiting shrubs for a prairie garden. They bloom profusely in spring, and bear heavy loads of dark red cherries. Their dainty white blossoms, shiny green leaves, and smooth, reddish bark appear similar to sour cherry tree cultivars, but dwarf sour cherries are hardier, shorter in stature, and less prone to suckering.

'Carmen Jewel' dwarf sour cherry blossoms

Sour cherry trees originated in eastern Europe, from natural hybrids of the sweet cherry tree (*Prunus avium*) and a hardy Mongolian cherry shrub (*Prunus fruticosa*). As the name implies, the tree bears tart fruit. Neither sweet nor sour cherry cultivars are prairie-hardy, with the exception of the 'Evans' sour cherry tree described in this chapter.

The dwarf sour cherry shrub is a unique crop that has been developed especially for the prairies (Agriculture Canada zone 2a) through breeding efforts that Les Kerr initiated at the Morden Research Centre, Manitoba, in the 1940s. He moved to Saskatoon, and continued crossing sour cherries with Mongolian cherries for forty years. His breeding stock was transferred to the University of Saskatchewan, where

Stewart Nelson, Rick Sawatzky, and Cecil Stushnoff were also working with sour cherries. The program continues today under the direction of Bob Bors, and the first dwarf sour cherry, 'SK Carmine Jewel,' was released in 1999. It was followed by five additional cultivars in 2003, known collectively as the "Romance" series. Each cultivar features slightly different attributes, along with staggered ripening times that stretch the sour cherry season from late July until early September.

The term "dwarf" describes the size of the plant, not the fruit. Many fruits are grafted on dwarfing rootstocks to make them easier to maintain and harvest, but dwarf sour cherries are grown on their own roots and are naturally short in stature.

How to Grow: Dwarf sour cherries are self-fruitful and only one plant is necessary to produce fruit, but you can extend the harvest if you plant cultivars that ripen at different times. Late-maturing cultivars are sweetest, as cooler nights result in higher sugar accumulation.

Fruit production begins three years after planting, and peak production is reached when the plant is about seven years old. Cherries are borne on wood from the previous season or older.

Dwarf sour cherries can be trained to a single trunk, although they are usually maintained as a large shrub, and pruned as described in Chapter

3. Allow weeping branches to remain, because they often hang from the weight of the fruit and continue to be productive.

To date, dwarf sour cherries have few pest problems, except deer. The plants are resistant to black knot fungus, which affects other related species.

Harvest: When ripe, both the skin and interior flesh turn a deep burgundy red that is almost black, and the fruit can be shaken right off the bush, although individually picked fruit is less likely to be damaged. If the plant is pruned into a tree, it must be picked by hand, not shaken. Resist

'Carmine Jewel' dwarf sour cherries

Immature fruit on 'Juliet' dwarf sour cherry shrub

the temptation to pick as soon as the fruits show colour; cherries become sweeter on the bush and will hang on for about three weeks after ripening. The fruit is tart, yet sweeter than the 'Evans' sour cherry.

Rinse cherries gently in cool water immediately after picking, and chill them before pitting. Remove the pits with a home cherry-pitter.

Serve: Dwarf sour cherries are superb in pies and juice. The maroon flesh produces a very dark juice, so there is no need to add the red food colouring that yellow-fleshed sour cherries require when making pie. Unlike many dark-coloured fruits, these cherries do not stain kitchen counters or clothing.

Preserve: Dry or freeze pitted cherries, or make preserves, juice, wine, or liqueur from them. Dried cherries taste fabulous combined with dark chocolate.

Suggested Cultivars

'Carmine Jewel' is the earliest to bear fruit and a favourite pie cherry. The fruit turns red in mid-July, ripens in late July, and becomes sweetest and almost black in August.

Romance Series

'Crimson Passion' produces the sweetest fruit and is favoured for fresh eating. It matures in mid-August. The plant can suffer dieback in harsh winters, and has the lowest suckering habit of the group.

'Cupid' produces the largest fruit and is the last variety to ripen, usually in late August to early September. It is one of the hardiest cultivars.

'Juliet' matures in early to mid-August, is considered sweet and a favourite for fresh eating, and has been described as the prettiest plant of the series, as well as one of the hardiest. It produces the largest fruit that can be accommodated in a commercial pitter.

'Romeo' looks similar to 'Carmine Jewel' and 'Juliet,' but ripens later, in late August to early September. Its cherries make good fresh eating, and are the best for juice. The plant can suffer dieback in harsh winters.

'Valentine' produces redder fruit than the other cultivars. It makes good pies. This cultivar is the most productive of the series, and one of the hardiest. It suckers slightly more than the others.

Cherry, Sour

Prunus cerasus 'Evans'
Family: rose (*Rosaceae*)
Type: deciduous tree
Height: 3.5 to 4.5 m (12 to 15 ft.)
Space: 3 to 4 m (10 to 14 ft.)
Light: full sun
Pollination: self-fruitful; only one plant is necessary

The 'Evans' cherry is a small tree that fits well in compact urban gardens. It features white flowers, glossy green leaves, peachy yellow fall colour, and

'Evans' sour cherries

'Evans' sour cherry tree

'Evans' sour cherry blossoms

mahogany red bark, and produces buckets of high quality bright red sour cherries in August. This tree is considered moderately hardy, to Agriculture Canada zone 3a, but is not as hardy as dwarf sour cherry shrubs.

The background of the 'Evans' cherry is a mystery. It was discovered growing in an Edmonton area home orchard that was planted in 1923. Ieuan Evans, a scientist with Alberta Agriculture, Food and Rural Development, recognized the potential of this hardy tree, and through his efforts during the 1980s, it was propagated and distributed throughout the prairies.

How to Grow: The 'Evans' cherry tree is self-fruitful and needs no other source of pollen. It grows vigorously and must be curtailed by withholding irrigation after the summer heat subsides in August to allow it to harden off. It is grown on its own roots and is usually pruned to a single trunk,

keeping the centre of the tree open to light and maintaining the size so the fruit can be reached. The tree sends out roaming suckers, which should be removed.

To guarantee your fair share of the crop, cover the tree with bird netting just as the cherries turn red. A mature tree produces so prolifically that it provides enough cherries for a family, as well as the birds.

Harvest: Harvest cherries in late August when the colour is bright red and the flavour is good. The tart fruit sweetens slightly on the tree and can be harvested over two to three weeks. Pick the cherries individually; do not try to shake them off the tree. Rinse the cherries after picking and chill them before removing the pits with a home cherry-pitter.

Serve: 'Evans' cherries have yellow flesh, similar to most sour cherry varieties, except the dwarf sour cherries from University of Saskatchewan. The fruit is excellent for making pies, jam, wine, and liqueur. Dried cherries are tart, but combine well with dark chocolate.

Preserve: Pitted cherries can be dried, frozen, or preserved in jam, juice, wine, or liqueur.

Crabapple

Malus spp.
Family: rose (*Rosaceae*)
Type: deciduous tree
Height: 5 to 10 m (15 to 30 ft.)
Space: 7 m (20 ft.)
Light: full sun
Pollination: cross-pollinated with another crabapple or apple cultivar

Crabapple trees are prized for their extravagant spring blossom display, which is a welcome sight after the bare branches of winter. Prairie crabapples are a result of crosses with the hardy Siberian crabapple (*Malus baccata*). Crabapples are distinguished from apples by fruit that is smaller than 5 cm (2 in.). Technically, the group is further split into crabapples and apple crabs, but generally the smaller fruit are called crabapples, and anything larger is considered to be an apple.

How to Grow: Two different crabapple cultivars are required for pollination and fruit. In urban areas, there is often another suitable crabapple or apple within range. Crabapples that are grown for fruit have white flowers; pink-flowered varieties, known as rosybloom crabapples, are cultivated as ornamental trees for their blossoms.

Crabapples are pruned like apples, emphasizing strong, horizontal branches. The trees can be extremely productive, and their fruit drop is messy if it is not harvested. Avoid locating a crabapple tree near high traffic or use areas such as a driveway, sidewalk, patio, or deck.

Harvest: Pick crabapples when they change to the colour appropriate for the variety, keeping the stem attached.

Serve: Even though the fruits are small, they can be eaten fresh. Crabapples are used for canning and baking, but are most valued for making jelly, juice, or liqueur. Crabapples should be processed immediately after picking.

Preserve: Crabapples make fabulous jelly and liqueur. Crabapple segments can be frozen (with the peel on) for later use in baking if you undertake the tedious task of cutting them off the cores in quarter sections.

Suggested Cultivars

'Dolgo' is an exceptionally hardy, ornamental tree with bright, almost fluorescent red oblong fruit produced in mid-season. Originally from a Russian seedling, it was introduced in 1917 through the

'Dolgo' crabapple flowers   'Dolgo' crabapples

South Dakota Agricultural Experimental Station in Brookings. It has moderate resistant to fire blight. The fruit ripens in early to mid-September and does not store long, but it makes an excellent deep red jelly.

'Kerr' was developed at the Morden Research Centre and introduced in 1952. It ripens after 'Rescue' and 'Dolgo,' in mid to late September. The dark purplish-red fruit is excellent for making juice, good for cooking, fair for eating, and stores well. The tree is very hardy and ornamental. It has a strong branching pattern and is resistant to fire blight.

'Rescue' was introduced in 1936 by the Experimental Farm in Scott, Saskatchewan. The tree is very hardy and ornamental with moderate resistance to fire blight. It produces sweet, light yellow fruit with red stripes that is good for fresh eating,

baking, or jelly. The fruit ripens early, in mid to late August, and has a very short shelf life.

Currant, Black
Ribes nigrum
Family: gooseberry (*Grossulariaceae*)
Type: deciduous shrub
Height: 1 to 1.5 m (3 to 5 ft.)
Space: 1.2 to 1.5 m (4 to 5 ft.)
Light: full sun to partial shade
Pollination: cross-pollinated; plant two different black currant cultivars

Although fresh black currants taste strong and musty, cooking the fruit with a bit of sugar transforms the flavour to rich, complex, and delicious. The plant has European roots and has been cultivated in Britain since the seventeenth century. Older cultivars have serious mildew problems, but the Scottish Crop Research Institute in Edinburgh, Scotland, has developed a group of hardy cultivars, known as

Black currant cultivars in the 'Ben' series are of superior quality.

the 'Ben' series, with improved disease resistance, productivity, and fruit quality.

Currants and gooseberries are related and share similar pest problems. The plants are alternate hosts for pine blister rust, an imported fungal disease that was lethal to white pines and the associated logging industry early in the twentieth century. In a futile attempt to control the disease, the United States placed a ban on currant and gooseberry cultivation. The federal ban was lifted in 1966, but confusion still exists regarding the legality of growing these species.

How to Grow: Choose and plant two different cultivars from the Scottish 'Ben' series with overlapping bloom times to get fruit. Black currants (*Ribes nigrum*) and red currants (*Ribes rubrum*) don't cross-pollinate with

each other. The best time to plant currants is very early in spring before the shrubs leaf out, from bare-root or container plants.

Black currants grow in partial shade, but full sun encourages the healthiest plants with high fruit yields, and reduces pest infestations. Avoid planting in low areas where frost pockets occur because the shrubs bloom very early in spring. Remove any flowers that are produced the first year to help the plants direct energy to getting established.

Currants are cool-climate plants that require evenly moist soil, especially in mid-summer to produce quality fruit. Keep the leaves dry while irrigating to prevent mildew. Black currants and red currants share similar pest problems (see the red currant description). Remove fruit that drops, as well as autumn leaves to reduce problems with insects and disease.

Black currants are produced on the previous year's growth. To keep the plant productive, prune the shrubs annually to remove branches that are over three years old. Aim to keep about eight strong branches. Do not prune the tips back, or fruit production will be reduced.

Harvest: Expect to harvest your first significant black currant crop the third year after planting. Allow the fruit to turn colour completely on the plant, and pick it as it starts to soften, but before it shrivels. It becomes sweeter on the bush. For jam, harvest the fruit slightly earlier, as the pectin levels are higher after it changes colour, but prior to softening. Harvest by pinching off individual fruits or fruit clusters. Chill harvested fruit immediately.

Serve: Black currants are not usually eaten fresh, unless you have acquired a taste for them, in which case the 'Ben Connan' and 'Ben Sarek' cultivars are deemed suitable. Black currants are more often made into sumptuous gourmet sauces, desserts, juice, wine, liqueur, and preserves, or used to flavour dairy products such as ice cream and yogurt.

Before using, black currants are "tipped and tailed" to remove dry remnants of the flowers. The fruit is frozen and then rolled around in a

plastic bag to knock off the unwanted parts. In some recipes, this step is unnecessary because the floral bits cook down with the fruits, but the stems should always be removed to prevent a "woody flavour."

Preserve: Freeze black currants whole or make them into jelly, jam, juice, wine, or liqueur.

Suggested Cultivars

'Ben Connan' is an early cultivar that suffers frost damage to its blossoms in some years. It produces large berries, has compact growth and is very productive and disease-resistant. The fruit are fabulous for making jams and can be eaten fresh if very ripe, but are not ideally suited for making juice.

'Ben Hope' is a mid-season cultivar that is productive and disease-resistant with vigorous, upright growth.

'Ben Sarek' is a mid-season cultivar that forms a compact plant of about 1 m (3 ft.) tall. It produces heavy yields of large berries that can be consumed fresh if very ripe. It has good frost tolerance and is resistant to rust and mildew.

'Ben Tirran' is late flowering, so it avoids frost damage, but late-maturing varieties appear to be preferred by the currant fruit fly. The plant has strong upright growth and produces high yields of large berries that are excellent for juice and jam.

Black currants

Currant, Red

Ribes rubrum

Family: gooseberry (*Grossulariaceae*)
Type: deciduous shrub
Height: 1.2 to 1.5 m (4 to 5 ft.)
Space: 1.2 to 1.5 m (4 to 5 ft.)
Light: full sun
Pollination: self-fruitful; only one plant is necessary

Red currant grows wild on the prairies, but garden cultivars originate from a European species that has been cultivated in Germany for over five hundred years. The plants produce clusters of bright red translucent berries in mid-summer that are excellent for making jelly, although you may need to cover the plants with bird net-

'Red Lake' red currants

ting to gather enough fruit. White and pink currants are red currant cultivars that lack pigment; the white is a nearly transparent albino form and the pink has clear skin and pink flesh.

In some regions, currant pest problems can frustrate all but the most enthusiastic gardeners, and the native currant fruit fly is particularly a nuisance. This small yellow fly with dark wing bands emerges as the plants are flowering and congregates on the underside of the leaves. Female flies lay eggs in the developing fruit; the maggots hatch and eat the fruit from the inside, causing the fruit to drop prematurely; then the pest overwinters in the soil below the plant. To prevent a build-up of this pest, it is essential to remove and dispose of fallen fruit on a daily basis.

Other bothersome pests include the imported currantworm and aphids. The currantworm is a sawfly larva that eats holes in the leaves, ultimately defoliating a shrub. Control these green worms early in the season by vigilant handpicking and squishing. Aphids also disfigure currant leaves, creating swollen red spots by sucking sap from underneath the foliage, but aphid damage usually affects the appearance of the leaves, not the fruit.

How to Grow: The plants are very hardy and self-fruitful. Only one plant is necessary to set fruit, although red currants are more productive with cross-pollination from two varieties.

The fruit is produced on spurs that grow from two- and three-year-old wood. Prune the shrubs annually to remove wood that is over three years old.

Harvest: Harvest red currants when they are bright red, picking the entire cluster at once to avoid damaging the fragile fruit. Chill harvested fruit immediately.

Preserve: Red currants are steamed to extract juice, and because of their seediness, are mainly used to make jelly.

Suggested Cultivars

'Honeywood Red' was selected by A. J. (Bert) Porter of Honeywood Nursery in Parkside, Saskatchewan. It produces large red berries in large clusters and is easily picked. Commercial availability of this cultivar is limited.

'Red Lake' is a Minnesota selection from 1933, and the most commonly grown cultivar. The fruit has good flavour and is produced in long clusters, which are easy to pick.

Gooseberry

Ribes oxyacanthoides
Family: gooseberry (*Grossulariaceae*)
Type: deciduous shrub
Height: 0.6 to 1.5 m (2 to 5 ft.)
Space: 1.2 to 1.5 m (4 to 5 ft.)
Light: full sun
Pollination: self-fruitful; only one plant is necessary

The gooseberry plant is uncommon in prairie gardens, even though one species is a prairie native, and it's thought that the climate of northern latitudes enhances the flavour of the fruit. Gooseberries are succulent, semi-transparent, grape-sized fruits that grow on dense thorny shrubs in Europe and North America. The fruit is popular in Europe, where it is cooked in luscious desserts. Older European gooseberry cultivars fell susceptible to pests and diseases in North American gardens, and when they were bred with native North American gooseberries to gain disease resistance, the resulting varieties had variable fruit quality. More recent cultivars from North American species, such as 'Jahn's Prairie,' have renewed interest in this humble fruit, and additional promising cultivars are in the testing stage and may soon be available commercially.

How to Grow: A gooseberry plant is self-fruitful; you need only one shrub to get fruit. Plant it as soon as the soil can be worked in spring. Full sun encourages high fruit yields, although gooseberries will tolerate partial afternoon shade.

The plants bear fruits on wood that is two and three years old. To maintain productivity, prune the shrub each year to remove wood that is more than three years old. Gooseberries and currants are related and share similar pest problems (see the red currant description).

'Hinnomaki Red' gooseberries

Harvest: Pluck individual gooseberries when the colour is appropriate for the variety, and the fruit begins to soften slightly. It becomes sweeter as it matures. Protect yourself from the thorns with leather gloves and long sleeves. Refrigerate harvested fruit immediately.

Serve: Gooseberries can be consumed fresh, but their delectable flavour is best in cooked desserts, pastries, or jam. Before using, the fruits are usually "tipped and tailed" to remove dry remnants of the flowers. Do this by freezing the fruits and rolling them around in a plastic bag to knock off the undesirable parts.

Preserve: Freeze berries or make gooseberry jam.

Suggested Cultivars

'Hinnomaki Red' and 'Hinnomaki Yellow' were developed in Finland from a European gooseberry species and released in 1950 and 1938, respectively. The variety name describes the fruit colour, and both produce quality fruit on hardy, disease-resistant plants.

'Jahn's Prairie' was selected from collections made in Alberta by Dr. Otto Jahn of Corvallis, Oregon, in 1984 and was released in 1996. It grows to a height of 1.5 m (5 ft.), is thorny, and is resistant to mildew and rust, as well as aphids and sawflies. It produces large yields of reddish-pink dessert-quality fruit that compares favourably with European cultivars that set the standard.

Grape

Vitis spp.

Family: grape (*Vitaceae*)
Type: deciduous vine
Height: 3 m (10 ft.)
Space: 2.5 m (8 ft.)
Light: full sun
Pollination: 'Valient' and 'Beta' are self-fruitful; only one plant is necessary, but other cultivars may need to be cross-pollinated with a different cultivar

It is believed that the first cultivated grapes arose from southwest Asia, and early records of making wine from grapes has been dated back 5500 years ago in western Iran. Plant breeders used native North American grapes to introduce hardiness into cultivated grapes, and the two hardiest cultivars, 'Valient' and 'Beta,' have cold-tolerant genes from the riverbank grape (*Vitis riparia*) that grows wild on the prairies. These cultivars produce small, sweet fruit that make fine table grapes, juice, and jelly. Newer, moderately hardy cultivars that require winter protection are grown here with varying degrees of success, and research is ongoing to develop good quality, hardy wine grapes that mature within our growing season.

How to Grow: 'Valient' and 'Beta' grapes are self-fruitful, but some grape cultivars need cross-pollination from a different cultivar. Grapes should be planted as dormant vines, in early spring, about two weeks before the final frost is expected.

Choose a sunny location, preferably south-facing for these heat-loving plants. The fruit quality is best when the vines are trained on a sturdy support to maximize exposure to sun and to keep the fruit clean. Grape vines are quite ornamental and easily guided over an arbour to provide a pleasant, leafy retreat from the hot summer sun. In an informal setting, the vines can be allowed to ramble over large boulders, which keep fruit off the ground and collect and radiate desirable warmth.

The rampant growth of grapevines is managed by pruning most of it off while the plant is dormant to achieve a

Grapevines should be pruned to control their rampant growth.

Grapevines require a sturdy support.

Ripe 'Valient' grapes

balance between growth and fruiting the following season. A practical approach is to prune such that four main vines grow out of a short trunk at the base of the plant in a fan-shaped fashion. The shoots should be tied to a sturdy trellis against a south wall, leaving enough space between the trellis and wall for air circulation.

To train your grapevine in this fashion, prune it immediately after planting to a single stem with two buds above the soil. As the buds sprout, tie both shoots to the trellis. After a heavy frost in the fall, cut the two vines back to two buds each. The following spring, shoots should sprout from each of the four buds. Tie all four shoots to the trellis, spreading

outward from the trunk like a fan. These stems, or canes, will serve as the main frame of your plant.

Every year, in March, prune each of the four canes back to a single bud, and allow each of the four buds to sprout and develop into new vines. (If pruning is done a few weeks later, as the buds swell, the plant will bleed sap, which can be disconcerting, but doesn't harm the plant). Remove any flower clusters that develop the first two years after planting and pinch off side shoots that sprout during the growing season. When the plant is in its third season, thin about one-third of the flower clusters, allowing the rest to develop grapes. Ripening can be hastened by pruning off the end of the vines, a few nodes out from the last fruit cluster, as the grapes noticeably swell.

Some gardeners keep tidy plants by pruning most of the growth off in autumn, after the leaves drop and a hard frost. If you adopt this strategy, keep the canes at least 60 cm (2 ft.) long with four to five buds on each cane throughout the winter. Continue the pruning cycle of cutting them back to a single bud the following spring as grapes are produced on the current season's growth. When the main structure ages and becomes brittle or non-productive, start a new set of canes from buds that originate near the base of the plant.

Young grapevines need consistently moist soil during the first month after planting. Continue to irrigate them

until late August, when water should be withheld to allow the plants to harden off. Irrigate them again deeply after the leaves drop, but before the ground freezes.

The cultivars 'Valiant' and 'Beta' can be grown with no winter protection, although mulching the canes helps prevent desiccation of next year's buds. Protect the plants by laying the canes down and covering them with 15 cm (6 in.) of soil, or by hilling soil around the base of the plant and its buds. In areas with reliable snow cover, the canes can simply be covered with mulch. Uncover the plant while it's still dormant in early spring and prune it.

Harvest: Allow grapes to develop colour completely, usually in early to

'Valient' grapevines provide a privacy screen.

mid-September and then taste them to determine when they are ripe. The fruit becomes sweeter on the vine and benefits from a light frost, but will deteriorate after additional frost. Support each cluster in your hand while snipping it from the vine with a shears. Refrigerate harvested fruit immediately.

Serve: Rinse grapes just before using them. Prairie hardy cultivars can be used fresh as table grapes, and are excellent for making juice or jelly. Store the fruit in plastic bags in the refrigerator for up to four days.

Preserve: Preserve grapes by making jelly or juice.

Suggested Cultivars

'Beta' was developed in Minnesota by crossing a 'Concord' grape with the native riverbank grape (*Vitis ripar-*

Honeyberry is a new fruit crop for prairie gardeners.
GLORIA GINGERA, PHOTO - UNIVERSITY OF SASKATCHEWAN

ia). It is very hardy and produces small, dark blue-black grapes.

'Valiant' is a very hardy cultivar that also has genes from the native riverbank grape. Bred at South Dakota University, it is earlier and hardier than 'Beta' and bears small, dark blue-purple grapes that are sweeter.

Honeyberry, Haskap, Edible Blue Honeysuckle

Lonicera caerulea
Family: honeysuckle (*Caprifoliaceae*)
Type: deciduous shrub
Height: 1.5 to 2 m (5 to 6.5 ft.)
Space: 1.5 to 2 m (5 to 6.5 ft.)
Light: full sun
Pollination: cross-pollinated; plant two different cultivars

Honeyberry is an exciting new fruit crop for prairie gardeners, with recent cultivars being bred and introduced by researchers at the University of Saskatchewan. It is known by other descriptive common names such as edible honeysuckle or blue honeysuckle, and in Japan it is considered a gourmet fruit, called haskap. The plant is native to wetlands of the Northern Hemisphere, including those of the Canadian Rockies and northern boreal forests of the Prairie Provinces. Research to develop better fruit has been ongoing in Japan and Russia for decades, and breeding has been in progress at University of Saskatchewan and Oregon State University since the

1990s. A few Canadian cultivars were developed during the 1940s, but these have bitter fruit; newer cultivars taste much better.

Honeyberries are large, rounded, non-suckering shrubs with dense, dark green foliage. The deep blue fruit looks like an oblong blueberry and has a pleasant flavour that is sweet, yet tart, with a hint of saskatoon and the texture of a grape. It is the earliest prairie fruit, and ripens about two weeks before the June-bearing strawberries.

How to Grow: Two honeyberry cultivars are necessary to set fruit, but not all cultivars are compatible with each other. As new cultivars emerge, trials are underway to determine which ones are compatible. The plant tolerates a wide range of soil conditions, and it's one of the few edible plants that can be grown in a low area where the soil does not drain well. Even though it blooms in very early spring, its inconspicuous yellow flowers seem unaffected by temperatures as low as -7°C (19°F).

The shrub begins bearing at a young age, usually in the second or third year. The plant must be covered with 1.25 cm (0.5 in.) bird netting as soon as the fruit shows colour, or birds will eat the entire crop. Raise the net off the shrub with stakes so that birds can't use it as a perch to eat from, and leave it in place for about four weeks, until the berries are harvested.

Honeyberries become dormant as summer heat sets in and the foliage can look a bit ratty at this time, except for the cultivar 'Borealis,' which retains a neat appearance. Maintain the plant by pruning it as described

Honeyberries

in Chapter 3. Honeyberry appears to have few pest or disease problems.

Harvest: Harvest honeyberries after the skin changes colour completely to a deep, waxy violet, and the flesh is reddish purple, not green. The fruit ripens uniformly and becomes sweeter on the shrub. Mature honeyberries will literally fall off the bush when touched. Harvest by picking individual fruits or by shaking the fruit-laden branches over a tarp. Chill harvested fruit immediately.

Serve: Honeyberries are excellent for eating fresh, or making juice, wine, pies, muffins, and jam. The fruit can be substituted in most recipes calling for blueberries, although honeyberries disintegrate more readily, and some recipes recommend reducing the sugar by half when making honeyberries into pie filling. The fruit also blends well in milk products to produce tasty shakes and ice cream.

Preserve: Freeze whole honeyberries, or make wine, juice, or jam.

Suggested Cultivars

'Berry Blue'™ is fast-growing and bears early-maturing, small fruit relative to other cultivars. It grows upright, reaching 1.8 m (6 ft.) and is recommended as a compatible polllinizer with 'Blue Belle,' 'Borealis,' and 'Tundra.'

'Blue Belle'™ is not as large or vigor-ous as 'Berry Blue.' It is a compact, weeping plant that reaches 0.9 to 1.2 m (3 to 4 ft.). It produces large fruit with good flavour and is a compatible pollinizer with 'Berry Blue.'

'Borealis' is a promising new cultivar released in 2007 by University of Saskatchewan, with parentage originating from the Kuril Islands located between Japan and Russia. It has large, sweet berries, good mildew resistance, and is considered one of the best tasting and most attractive cultivars. It is 1.5 m (5 ft.) tall and wide. It is not compatible with 'Tundra.' 'Berry Blue' is currently recommended as a pollinizer.

'Tundra' is a 2007 release from University of Saskatchewan, also with plant genes from the Kuril Islands in its ancestry. It has durable fruit, with excellent flavour, is suitable for commercial harvesting, and is slightly smaller than 'Borealis.' It is not compatible with 'Borealis.' Currently, 'Berry Blue' is recommended as a pollinizer.

Pear

Pyrus spp.
Family: rose (*Rosaceae*)
Type: deciduous tree
Height: 5 to 8 m (16 to 26 ft.)
Space: 5 to 8 m (16 to 26 ft.)
Light: full sun
Pollination: cross-pollinated; plant two different cultivars

'Ure' pear blossoms

Pears are highly ornamental trees with showy white flowers, glossy, deep green leaves, and copper autumn colour. Research is ongoing to improve the fruit quality, as prairie-hardy cultivars produce small pears that tend to become gritty quickly after they mature. Some feel that these are best suited for preserves, but if you monitor ripening closely and pick them at just the right stage, the fruit can be smooth and luscious. Many gardeners accept the shortcomings of the fruit and enjoy pear trees for their sheer beauty.

How to Grow: Two different pear cultivars are necessary for fruit production. The ornamental Ussurian pear (*Pyrus ussuriensis*) can also supply compatible pollen. Since pears bloom early, it is easier to cultivate them in the sheltered microclimate of urban areas.

Pear trees mature slowly and take six years or longer to begin bearing fruit. Fruit production can be heavy, so avoid planting a pear in traffic high use areas where the fruit drop will be a nuisance. The fruit is produced on short spurs that form on wood that is two years and older. Thin the fruit according to the method described in Chapter 3 to increase fruit quality and minimize the strain of heavy bearing on the tree.

Pear trees have an upright form and should be pruned to maintain one central trunk, lightly thinning the branches and removing any suckers from the base each year.

Harvest: Pick pears when they reach their mature size, while the fruit is still hard, as the seeds begin to turn brown. The fruit stalk should separate from the tree without difficulty as you support the fruit and twist it, taking care not to damage the spur.

Allow pears to ripen at room temperature, and taste them to test when they are ready to eat. They are very perishable and only last a few days once ripe.

Serve: Some prairie-hardy cultivars make good fresh eating, or they can be poached, used in baking or preserves.

Preserve: Pears can be canned or made into jam or liqueur.

'Ure' pears

Suggested Cultivars

'Earligold' is a very hardy selection of a 'Ure' seedling, released by Jeffries Nursery in Portage la Prairie, Manitoba. It is a large, vigorous, pyramid-shaped tree that reaches 8 m (26 ft.) tall and wide. The fruit is similar to 'Ure.'

'Golden Spice' is a moderately hardy variety introduced by the University of Minnesota in 1949. The fruit is slightly tart and described as spicy. The tree is about 8 m (26 ft.) tall with a 5 m (16 ft.) spread.

'John' is a selection from University of Saskatchewan, bred by Cecil Patterson and released as part of a very hardy pear series dubbed the "apostle pears." It produces the largest fruit of the prairie pears, similar in shape to a commercial pear, and is good for fresh eating and preserves. The tree is more robust and faster growing than the 'Thomas' cultivar of the same series, at 7 m (23 ft.) tall and 4 m (13 ft.) wide.

'Thomas' is a very hardy selection, released in 1960, as part of the "apostle pears" series developed by Cecil Patterson at University of Saskatchewan. It bears round fruit and is recommended as the best tasting pear of the two hardiest types, although the fruit is very firm when ripe. The tree is round-headed and about 6 m (20 ft.) tall and 4 m (13 ft.) wide.

'Ure' is a popular Morden Research Centre release from 1978. Of the cultivars listed here, it produces the best quality fruit for fresh eating, although it has a short shelf life and quickly becomes gritty. Its 5 cm (2 in.) pears look and taste like a 'Bartlett,' only they are smaller. The fruit is also good for canning. This tree reaches 5 m (16 ft.) tall and 4 m (13 ft.) wide. It is moderately hardy, and best suited to zone 3a or warmer.

Plum

Prunus spp.

Family: rose (*Rosaceae*)
Type: deciduous tree
Height: 3.5 to 4 m (12 to 14 ft.)
Space: 3 to 4 m (10 to 14 ft.)
Light: full sun
Pollination: cross-pollinated; two different Asian plum cultivars will cross-pollinate each other, but hybrid plums require a wild plum pollinizer.

It's fortunate that plum trees are small, as the secret to producing a sweet, juicy plum is having two compatible cultivars close to each other for cross-pollination. Plums produce lacy clouds of white blossoms early in the season while frost still threatens and few pollinators are about. In addition to these crop-limiting conditions, plums are very particular about their pollen source. To set fruit, plums need to receive pollen from a different but compatible cultivar with an overlapping bloom time, and it has taken time to sort out which prairie-hardy

Plums bloom very early in spring.   A native plum is necessary to pollinate hybrid plums.

cultivars are actually compatible with each other.

Prairie-hardy plum cultivars fall into two categories: Asian and hybrids. Asian plums, also known as Japanese plums, are made up of cultivars from an Asian species (*Prunus salicina*). Canadian and American breeders developed the hardier hybrid plums by crossing Asian cultivars with two wild prairie plums: the Canada plum (*Prunus nigra*) and the American plum (*Prunus americana*). The two North American native species are similar in appearance and their distribution range almost completely overlaps, except the Canada plum is found slightly further north and the American plum extends much further south. Wild plums produce small fruits that are great for jam, but recent findings show that these trees are also valuable as pollen sources to the cultivated varieties.

It has been shown that an Asian plum will bear fruit if it is cross-pollinated with either a different Asian plum cultivar or a wild plum that blooms at the same time. Hybrid plums will set fruit only if they receive pollen from a pure wild Canada or American plum, not another hybrid plum. At present, very few nurseries stock wild plums, but work is underway to improve their availability. Wild plum cultivars such as 'Bounty' and 'Dandy' are not effective, and it has been determined that they are probably not entirely wild and likely have Asian genes in their background.

Other pollinizers (plants that provide compatible pollen) have been suggested for the hybrid plum, and contrary to information that is widely distributed, none has proven effective. Sour cherries and Nanking cherries (*Prunus tomentosa*) are not compatible with hybrid plums. Western sandcherries (*Prunus pumila* var. *besseyi*) are compatible, but they bloom too late to pollinate hybrid plums effectively. Cherryplums (hybrids between Asian plums and western sandcherries) bloom later than most hybrid plums and are probably ineffective pollinizers.

How to Grow: To optimize your crop potential, plant two different but compatible plum cultivars as close as possible (allowing space to maintain mature trees). If your chosen plum is a hybrid cultivar, seek a pure wild plum

'Pembina' plums

to pollinate it from a knowledgeable prairie fruit grower. Plant both plum trees on the same side of the house to ensure an overlapping bloom period since each area of the garden warms up at a different rate.

Anther plum production obstacle is that wild plums bloom later than early-blooming hybrids and Asian plums. It's possible to encourage your wild plum to bloom earlier by train-ing the lower branches to grow close to the ground or a sunny wall, where they receive warmth radiating from the surface. Tie young branches or pin them in place if necessary. A plum tree blooms from its base upwards, and extra warmth may encourage the lower stems to flower early enough to overlap with the early-blooming hy-brids and Asian plums. The middle of the tree will naturally bloom about the same time as mid-season hybrids, and the upper branches will bloom with the late-flowering hybrids.

Plums are produced on spurs that are two to eight years old and on short shoots. Keep your tree productive by removing about 30 cm. (12 in.) of the previous year's growth each spring. Thin competing or excessive branches to maintain the central leader, and remove sprouts at the base, as they are susceptible to fire blight entry.

All cultivars listed here are very hardy and produce good plums for fresh eating.

Harvest: Allow plums to ripen on the tree to fully develop flavour, as the fruit becomes softer, but not sweeter after harvest. Pick plums gently from the spurs, when the skin changes to the appropriate colour for the variety and the fruit feels just slightly soft. Store plums at room temperature or refrigerated; they last only a few days.

Serve: Hybrid and Asian plums are delicious fresh or used in baking,

canning, or made into jam. Tart, wild plums are valued for making jam and sauce, and are reported to be sweeter after a light frost.

Preserve: Pit plums, then freeze or dry them or make them into jam.

Suggested Cultivars
Hybrid plums (must plant with a pure wild plum)
'Patterson Pride' is a late-season hybrid with deep red 4 to 5 cm (1.5 to 2 in.) fruit of excellent quality. The tree has a weeping growth habit. It was bred by Cecil Patterson and introduced in 1960 by University of Saskatchewan.

'Pembina' is a popular mid-season hybrid, bred by Niels Hansen and introduced in 1917 by South Dakota University. It bears large 5 cm (2 in.) fruit that is red with a waxy bloom, and of excellent quality.

'Prairie' is a mid-season plum, very similar to 'Pembina,' bred by Cecil Patterson and introduced in 1960 by University of Saskatchewan. It was selected from a seedling, and since plums are capable of producing seedlings that have not been fertilized with pollen from another plant, it has been speculated that this plant may be genetically identical to 'Pembina.'

Asian plums (plant with a different Asian cultivar or a pure wild plum)
'Brookgold' is an early Asian plum, introduced in 1979 by the Crop Diversification Centre South in Brooks, Alberta. It bears golden yellow fruit with a reddish splash.

'Ivanovka' is an early Asian cultivar that produces a yellowish plum, splashed with red. Introduced by the Morden Research Station in 1939, it's slightly less hardy than the other cultivars listed here, but is still considered very hardy, and its good flavour makes it worth growing.

'Ptitsin #3' is a Morden Research Centre introduction and one of the hardiest Asian plums. It bears yellow-green fruit early in the season.

'Ptitsin #5' is a very hardy Morden Research Centre introduction with yellow-green fruit early in the season. It is smaller than 'Ptitsin #3,' but has good flavour.

Saskatoon, Serviceberry
Amelanchier alnifolia
Family: rose (*Rosaceae*)
Type: deciduous shrub
Height: up to 5.5 m (18 ft.)
Space: 1 to 2 m (3 to 6.5 ft.)
Light: full sun to partial shade
Pollination: self-fruitful; only one plant is necessary

Saskatoons grow wild across the prairies, and foraging for ripe fruit is a summer ritual for many prairie residents. The plant is striking as it becomes enveloped in snowy white flowers in early spring, especially when

Saskatoon flowers

'Thiessan' saskatoon plants grow quite tall.

it is planted near golden currant (*Ribes aureum*), another native shrub with edible fruit that displays a mass of yellow blossoms at the same time. Saskatoon cultivars are extremely hardy, and have been selected from superior plants in the wild, not through conventional breeding. Those listed here produce exceptional fruit.

How to Grow: Only one cultivar is necessary as saskatoons are self-fruitful. Although the plants are native, regular irrigation during fruit development is necessary to produce quality fruit. Two to four years after planting, the plants bear fruit on wood that is one-year-old or older, with the largest berries borne on one- and two-year-old wood. Some varieties, such as 'Honeywood' and 'Northline' become

productive earlier than others.

Saskatoon plants grow quite tall, and it's easier to harvest the fruit if you keep the plant at a height of 2 m (6.5 ft.). Maintain good productivity and air circulation by removing low, spreading branches and older branches from the centre of the plant.

Like many native prairie shrubs, saskatoon sends out suckers that should be removed or the plant will eventually form a thicket. These suckers can be used to obtain new plants, by digging them and removing them from the parent plant in early spring. Replant sprouts at the original depth, keeping the soil moist until roots have established.

Saskatoons usually fruit satisfactorily in a home garden, although the plant can suffer damage from pests such as saskatoon bud moth, saskatoon sawfly, and the woolly elm aphid, and it is an alternate host for the fungal disease, juniper/saskatoon rust. Minimize pest problems by maintaining healthy plants and vigilantly cleaning up fallen fruit and autumn leaves. Control the rust fungus on junipers by pruning as described in Chapter 3.

Harvest: Saskatoons mature in July and August. Pick the fruit when it turns very deep purple, but still shows some red, or at the stage you prefer the flavour. As the fruit ripens to purplish black, it becomes less astringent.

Rinse saskatoons by immersing them in cold water, allowing the debris to float to the top. Let the fruit dry and store it in a covered container in the refrigerator for up to four days.

Serve: Fresh saskatoons are a true prairie treat, and make great pies and jam.

Preserve: Freeze the fruit or make it into jam.

Suggested Cultivars

'Honeywood' was introduced in 1973, by A. J. (Bert) Porter of Honeywood Nurseries in Parkside, Saskatchewan. It blooms a few days later than other varieties, begins bearing at an early age, and produces good yields of large fruit that ripen unevenly. The plant reaches a height of 2 to 3 m (6.5 to 10 ft.) with few suckers.

'JB 30' is a selection from Jarvis Blushke of Blue Sky Farm in Langham, Saskatchewan, and trialed at University of Saskatchewan. It bears good yields of large fruit, similar to 'Thiessen,' but with a stronger flavour and uniform ripening. It is a compact plant at 2.2 m (7.5 ft.) with few suckers, which makes it ideal for small gardens.

'Martin' is from a 'Thiessen' seedling, selected by Dieter Martin of Langham, Saskatchewan. It has large fruit and uniform ripening. The plant reaches a height of 2.5 m (8 ft.) and suckers moderately.

'Northline' was introduced in 1960 by John Wallace of Beaverlodge, Alberta. It is a relatively short plant, 1.5 to 1.8 m (5 to 6 ft.) that produces early, but it suckers vigorously.

'Thiessen' is favoured for the flavour of its large fruit that ripens over an extended period. It is early blooming and may be touched by frost. It is a rangy, upright shrub, 4 to 5 m (13 to 16 ft.) tall with moderate suckering. It was discovered on the Isaak Thiessen family farm in 1906 near Waldheim, Saskatchewan, and introduced in 1972 by Lakeshore Nurseries of Saskatoon.

'Honeywood' saskatoon fruit

Index of Seed and Plant Sources

The intent of this list is to provide a range of seed and plant sources for Canadian and American home gardeners. It is not intended to be comprehensive, or as an endorsement of any of the companies or their products.

Canada

Alberta Nurseries, Bow Seed
<www.gardenersweb.ca>

Boughen Nurseries
<www.boughennurseries.net>

Boundary Garlic
<www.garlicfarm.ca>

Bow Point Nursery Ltd.
<www.bowpointnursery.com>

The Cottage Gardener
<www.cottagegardener.com>

Dominion Seed House
<www.dominion-seed-house.com>

Eagle Creek Seed Potatoes
<www.seedpotatoes.ca>

Early's Farm & Garden Centre
<www.earlysgarden.com>

Haskap Central Sales
<www.haskapcentral.com>

Hole's Greenhouses and Gardens
<www.holesonline.com>

Jeffries Nurseries
<www.jeffriesnurseries.com>

Lindenberg Seeds
<www.lindenbergseeds.ca>

Mapple Farm
<www.mapplefarm.com>

McFayden Seed Co. Ltd
<www.mcfayden.com>

Ontario Seed Company (OSC Seeds)
<www.oscseeds.com>

Prairie Garden Seeds
<www.prseeds.ca>

Prairie Tech Propagation
<www.prairietechpropagation.com>

Richters Herb Specialists
<www.richters.com>

Sage Garden Herbs
<www.herbs.mb.ca>

Salt Spring Seeds
<www.saltspringseeds.com>

Spring Arbour Farm
<www.springarbourfarm.com>

Stokes Seeds
<www.stokeseeds.com>

T & T Seeds
<www.ttseeds.com>

Terra Edibles
<www.terraedibles.ca>

Veseys Seeds
<www.veseys.com>

West Coast Seeds
<www.westcoastseeds.com>

William Dam Seeds
<www.damseeds.com>

United States

Abundant Life Seeds
<www.abundantlifeseeds.com>

W. Atlee Burpee Seed Co
<www.burpee.com>

The Cook's Garden
<www.cooksgarden.com>

Gardens Alive
<www.gardensalive.com>

Gourmet Seed International
<www.gourmetseed.com>

Heirloom Seeds
<www.heirloomseeds.com>

High Altitude Gardens, Seeds Trust
<www.seedstrust.com>

Irish Eyes, Garden City Seeds
<www.irish-eyes.com>

Johnny's Selected Seeds
<www.johnnyseeds.com>

J.W. Jung Seed Co
<www.jungseed.com>

Kitchen Garden Seeds
<www.kitchengardenseeds.com>

Kitazawa Seed Co.
<www.kitazawaseed.com>

New England Seed Company
<www.neseed.com>

Nichols Garden Nursery
<www.nicholsgardennursery.com>

Pinetree Garden Seeds
<www.superseeds.com>

Renee's Garden Seeds
<www.reneesgarden.com>

Ronninger Potato Farm LLC
<www.ronningers.com>

Seed Saver's Exchange
<www.seedsavers.org>

Southmeadow Fruit Gardens
<www.southmeadowfruitgardens.com>

Stokes Seeds, Inc.
<www.stokeseeds.com>

Territorial Seed Company
<www.territorialseed.com>

Vermont Bean Seed Company
<www.vermontbean.com>

Wood Prairie Farm
<www.woodprairie.com>

References

Allan, Ken, 1998. *Sweet Potatoes for the Home Garden: With Special Techniques for Northern Growers*. Kingston, ON: Green Spade Books.

Ashworth, Suzanne, 2002. *Seed to Seed: Seed Saving and Growing Techniques for Vegetable Gardeners*, 2nd edition. Decorah, IA: Seed Savers Exchange, Inc.

Bantle, Jackie, 2009. "Winter Squash," *The Gardener for the Prairies*, 15(4). Saskatoon, SK: The Saskatchewan Gardeners, Inc.

Barkley, Shelley, 1999. *Alberta Yards & Gardens: What to Grow*. Edmonton, AB: Alberta Agriculture, Food and Rural Development.

Bennet, Jennifer, 2002. *Lilacs for the Garden*. Willowdale, ON: Firefly Books Ltd.

Bors, Bob and Rick Sawatzky, 2000. "Dwarf Sour Cherries for the Prairies," *The Gardener for the Prairies* 6 (2). Saskatoon, SK: The Saskatchewan Gardeners, Inc.

Bors, Bob and Linda Matthews, 2004. *Dwarf Sour Cherries: A Guide for Commercial Production*. Saskatoon, SK: University Extension Press.

Bors, Bob, 2005. "Blue Honeysuckle," *The Gardener for the Prairies* 11 (4). Saskatoon, SK: The Saskatchewan Gardeners, Inc.

Bors, Bob, Rick Sawatzky and Clarence Peters, 2007. *Popular Fruit Varieties, 2007*, (http://www.usask.ca/agriculture/plantsci/dom_fruit/articles.html). Saskatoon, SK: University of Saskatchewan, Department of Plant Sciences/Saskatchewan Agriculture, Food and Rural Revitalization.

Bryan, Nora & Ruth Staal, 2003. *The Prairie Gardener's Book of Bugs: A Guide to Living with Common Garden Insects*. Calgary, AB: Fifth House Publishers.

Bubel, Nancy, 1988. *The New Seed-Starters Handbook*. Emmaus, PA: Rodale Press.

Canadian Farm Business Management Council, 2002. *Introduction to Certified Organic Farming*, second edition. Ottawa, ON.

Chalker-Scott, Linda, 2008. *The Informed Gardener*. Seattle, WA: University of Washington Press.

Coleman, Eliot, 1992. *The New Organic Grower's Four Season Harvest: how to harvest fresh organic vegetables from your home garden all year long.* Post Mills, VT: Chelsea Green Publishing Company.

Creasy, Rosalind, 1999. *The Edible Flower Garden.* Boston, MA: Periplus Editions (HK) Ltd.

Cutler, Karen Davis, 1997. *The Complete Vegetable and Herb Gardener: A Guide to Growing Your Garden Organically.* Hoboken, NJ: Wiley Publishing.

Daku, Allan B., 1997. "Bert Porter's Bush Fruit," *The Gardener for the Prairies* 3 (4). Saskatoon, SK: The Saskatchewan Gardeners, Inc.

Davis, J.G. and P. Kendall, 2005. "Preventing *E. coli* From Garden to Plate," no. 9.369. Fort Collins, CO: Colorado State University Extension-Nutrition Resources.

Eck, Joe, 2005. *Elements of Garden Design.* New York, NY: North Point Press.

Engeland, Ron L., 1991. *Growing Great Garlic: The Definitive Guide for Organic Gardeners and Small Farmers.* Okanogan, WA: Filaree Productions.

England, Ray, 2007. "Wild Plums in the Old Northwest," *The Prairie Garden: The Edible Landscape*, 68th Annual Edition. Winnipeg, MB: The Prairie Garden Committee.

Evans, Ieuan R., 1997. "The 'Evans' Cherry," *The Gardener for the Prairies*, 3 (1). Saskatoon, SK: The Saskatchewan Gardeners, Inc.

Fedor, John, 2001. *Organic Gardening for the 21st Century.* Pleasantville, NY: Reader's Digest.

Flanagan, June, 2005. *Native Plants for Prairie Gardens.* Calgary, AB: Fifth House Publishers.

Flanagan, June, 2004. "Melons from an Alberta garden," *Alberta Gardener*, 3 (4). Winnipeg, MB: Pegasus Publications Inc.

Fry, Ken, Doug Macaulay and Don Williamson, 2008. *Garden Bugs of Alberta: Gardening to Attract, Repel and Control.* Edmonton, AB: Lone Pine Publishing.

Gillman, Jeff, 2008. *The Truth about Garden Remedies: What Works, What Doesn't and Why.* Portland, OR: Timber Press.

Gillman Jeff, 2008. *The Truth about Organic Gardening: Benefits, Drawbacks, and the Bottom Line.* Portland, OR: Timber Press.

Hartmann, Hudson T. and Dale E. Kester, 1975. *Plant Propagation Principles and Practices*, 3rd Ed. Englewood Cliffs, NJ: Prentice-Hall Inc.

Hole, Lois, 1993. *Lois Hole's Vegetable Favorites*. Edmonton, AB: Lone Pine Publishing.

Howard, Ronald J., J. Allan Garland and W. Lloyd Seaman, editors, 1994. *Diseases and Pests of Vegetable Crops in Canada: an illustrated compendum*. Ottawa, ON: The Canadian Phytopathological Society and Entomological Society of Canada.

Hrycan, William, 2007. "Pears for the Prairie Garden," *The Gardener*, 13 (1). Saskatoon, SK: The Gardener for the Prairies Inc.

Kuepper, George and Kevin Everett, 2007. "Potting Mixes for Certified Organic Production," Fayetteville, AR: ATTRA-National Sustainable Agriculture Information Service, (http://attra.ncat.org/attra-pub/potmix.html), NCAT/USDA-RBS.

Larkcom, Joy, 2004. *Creative Vegetable Gardening*. London, England: Mitchell Beazley.

Manitoba Agriculture, Food and Rural Initiatives, 2006. "Crops: Strawberry Cultivars,"<http://www.gov.mb.ca/agriculture/crops/fruit/blb01s19.html>.

Matthews, Linda, 2007. "New Small Fruit Crops for the Prairies," *The Gardener for the Prairies*, 13 (4). Saskatoon, SK: The Gardener for the Prairies Inc.

Nardi, James B., 2007. *Life in the Soil: A Guide for Naturalists and Gardeners*. Chicago, IL: The University of Chicago Press.

Patent, Dorothy Hinshaw and Diane E. Bilderback, 1991. *The Harrowsmith Country Life Book of Garden Secrets: a down-to-earth guide to the art and science of growing better vegetables*. Charlotte, VT: Camden House Publishing, Inc.

Philip, Hugh & Ernest Mengersen, 1989. *Insect Pests of the Prairies*. Edmonton, AB: University of Alberta Press.

Porter, Brian, 2002. "The Neglected Gooseberry," *The Gardener for the Prairies*, 8 (2). Saskatoon, SK: The Saskatchewan Gardeners, Inc.

Porter, Brian, 2003. "Currants," *The Gardener for the Prairies*, 9 (1). Saskatoon, SK: The Saskatchewan Gardeners, Inc.

Prance, Sir Ghillean, Consulting Editor, 2005. *The Cultural History of Plants*. New York, NY: Routledge.

Proulx, E. Annie, 1985. *The Fine Art of Salad Gardening*. Emmaus, PA: Rodale Press.

Quinty, F. and L. Rochefort, 2003. Peatland Restoration Guide, second edition. Quebec City, PQ: Canadian Sphagnum Peat Moss Association and New Brunswick Department of Natural Resources and Energy (http://www.gret-perg.ulaval.ca).

Reich, Lee, 2010. *The Pruning Book*, 2nd ed. Newton, CT: Taunton Press.

Sawatzky, Rick, *Plums on the Prairies*. Saskatoon, SK: University of Saskatchewan Plant Sciences, (www.usask.ca/agriculture/plantsci/dom_fruit/articles.html).

Shaw, Tom, managing editor, 1986. *University of Alberta Home Gardening Course*. Edmonton, AB: University of Alberta Faculty of Extension.

Skinner, Hugh, 2007. "Eastern Asia's Contribution to Hardy Fruit Development: The Common & the Exotic," *The Prairie Garden: The Edible Landscape*, 68th Annual Edition. Winnipeg, MB: The Prairie Garden Committee.

Swiader, John M. and George W. Ware, 2002. *Producing Vegetable Crops*, Fifth Edition. Danville, IL: Interstate Publishers.

Thorness, Bill, 2009. *Edible Heirlooms: heritage vegetables for the maritime garden*. Seattle, WA: Skipstone.

Vaillancourt, Gerard, 1994. *Backyard Pest Management in Alberta*. Edmonton, AB: Alberta Agriculture, Food and Rural Development.

Waterer, Doug, 2004. "Potatoes," *The Gardener for the Prairies*, 10 (2). Saskatoon, SK: The Saskatchewan Gardeners, Inc.

Williams, Sara, 2006. *In a Cold Land: Saskatchewan's Horticultural Pioneers*. Saskatoon, SK: Grasswood Books and the Saskatchewan Perennial Society.

Index